CHAOS TO COSMOS
Studies in Biblical Patterns
of Creation

SCHOLARS PRESS
Studies in the Humanities

CHAOS TO COSMOS
Studies in Biblical Patterns of Creation

by

Susan Niditch

Scholars Press
Atlanta, Georgia

CHAOS TO COSMOS
Studies in Biblical Patterns of Creation

by

Susan Niditch

Cover Graphic:
Jewish illuminated manuscript of Adam and Eve,
end of the 13th century

Library of Congress Cataloging in Publication Data

Niditch, Susan.
    Chaos to cosmos
    (Scholars Press studies in the humanities series ; no. 6)
    I. Bible. O.T. Genesis I-XI—Criticism, interpretation,
etc. I. Title. II. Series.
BS1235.2.N47 1984 22'.1106   84-13846
ISBN: 0-89130-762-1
ISBN: 0-89130-763-X (pbk.)

Printed in the United States of America
on acid-free paper

For my dear ones,
Robert and Rebecca

CONTENTS

Acknowledgements

This book took shape over the course of several years but crystallized as a result of my participation in the Introduction to Liberal Studies Program at Amherst College. The interdisciplinary course, "In Search of Paradise," was team-taught with my colleague Professor Barry O'Connell whose critical insight and wide-ranging expertise honed my own thinking. I wish to thank him as well as the fine students who studied with us. The final chapter of this work on early Christianity owes much to the influence of my dear husband, Robert Doran, the New Testament scholar of the family. He has unfolded for me a creative and exciting way of reading Paul. Several people have read the manuscript, offering valuable suggestions: Dr. Cynthia Thompson; Professor Albert B. Lord; Professor Edgar Slotkin; and Professor John Pemberton, III.

I thank Amherst College for the leave time in which to write and for a research grant which aided in preparation of the manuscript. The manuscript was typed expertly and graciously by Diane Beck. Finally, I thank Conrad Cherry for his confidence in the work and Gene M. Tucker for his careful and caring reading.

Introduction

The search for the origins of the universe is ultimately a search for self, and if we believe Freud, the search for the unconscious self begins with the study of our primal myths. Both searches—for origins and for self—are universal and have existed as long as humans have existed as cultural beings. One might suggest that these searches no longer involve the rich narrative traditions we call myths, that humans no longer express their deepest values and most profound fears, their explanations of reality and their adjustments to it, in shared stories, authorless, ahistorical, archetypal, and richly symbolical. One might assume that the searches for origins and for self now continue only in the realm of scientific inquiry, the purview of psychoanalysis or physics or genetics. Such an assumption, however, is wrong. Human beings continue to find meaning in new myths or to resurrect and revitalize the old ones.

This study investigates how the Hebrew myths of chaos, creation, and cosmos have informed the lives of various generations and how in the process the myths themselves have been transformed and renewed.

Genesis 1–11 is an especially informative and inclusive corpus of myths. In a short space it deals not only with the becoming of the universe and with mankind's place in the universe, but also with the networks of relationships that exist among people. All too often Genesis 1–11 is approached by Bible scholars solely as a revealer of the human being's relationship with God, but students of other disciplines might well approach these narratives with different questions and emphases.

Were a native informant to tell an anthropologist a tale about a first couple's ideal existence in a garden and the events by which they are expelled to a real world of frustrating work and pain, the anthropologist might ask himself, what kind of a society does this tale reflect? Are there hints in it as to how the society functions, about interrelationships among individuals and between groups? Are certain categories reinforced by the tale, categories with implications for the native's view of himself or his society's view of itself? A psychologist upon hearing this myth might ask, what human emotions and needs are fulfilled by such a tale and revealed by it? Are certain subconscious tensions and ambivalences implicit in the tale or resolved by it? The philosophical student of religion might ask how such a tale makes suffering bearable. Does the tale explain existence in some sense or resolve its paradoxes? Questions such as these are relevant and enriching. All too often the Bible scholar discussing Genesis 3 concentrates only on issues of sin and punishment, the limits God sets upon humans and their disobedience.[1]

---

[1] I do not mean to imply that all Bible scholars have ignored the possibilities offered by the approaches of other disciplines. There has been a marked interest of late in the application of what broadly might be termed structuralist literary criticism to a variety of biblical texts with special attention paid to Genesis 2–3. The various types of structuralist analysis are outlined neatly by Daniel Patte in *Genesis 2 and 3. Kaleidoscopic Structural Readings* (*Semeia* 18 [1980]) 7–22. For a discussion and application of French structuralist approaches see Robert M. Polzin, *Biblical Structuralism. Method and Subjectivity in the Study of Ancient Texts* (*Missoula, MT*: Scholars Press, 1977); for a recent application of Proppian Russian formalism see Jack M. Sasson, *Ruth: A Translation with a Philological Commentary and a Formalist-Folklorist Interpretation* (Baltimore: John Hopkins, 1979); for a recent study in rhetorical criticism see Phyllis Trible, *God and the Rhetoric of Sexuality* (Philadelphia: Fortress, 1978). Recent studies of Genesis 2–3 employing the "new" methodologies include Joel W. Rosenberg, "The Garden Story Forward and Backward. The non-narrative dimension of Genesis 2–3," *Prooftexts* 1 (1981) 1–27, and the collection of essays in Daniel Patte, *Genesis 2 and 3.* This collection includes new essays and reworkings of essays presented at the 1978 meetings of the Society of Biblical Literature and published in the *SBL Seminar Papers*, Vol. 1, 31–69. A well-known and controversial earlier study is Edmund Leach's *Genesis as Myth and Other Essays* (London: Jonathan Cape, 1969) 7–23. See the critique by J. A. Emerton, "An Examination of a Recent Structuralist Interpretation of Genesis XXXVIII," *VT* (1976) 79–98. For a study with interesting structuralist nuances see M. Fishbane, *Text and Texture* (New York: Schocken, 1979) 3–39.

Two considerations guide this study in the hopes of gaining new insight into Genesis 1–11 and the use of its mythology in on-going tradition. First, Genesis 1–11 is to be respected as literature, treated as a composition made of many narrative themes each of which has a definable structure of content and various levels of meaning. These themes, which are characterized by particular patterns of content, can be compared to one another and to the literary creations of other cultures. Second is an acknowledgement that the patterns of sacred texts are integrally related to the patterns of human lives. The themes of Genesis 1–11 reflect realities and help to shape them. The first consideration is literary-critical, the second, anthropological. Both imply an approach which is inter-disciplinary and cross-cultural.

The literary-critical approaches and interests of this study find a background in the work of A. B. Lord and David E. Bynum, scholars of comparative literature and more specifically of early and oral literatures.[2] Albert Lord's most famous work has involved the study of Homer's *Iliad* and *Odyssey* in the light of Serbo-Croatian epics, collected and recorded by him and his teacher Milman Parry. Lord has suggested that the *Iliad* and the *Odyssey* were composed orally by a bardic performer who weaved his tale extemporaneously in accordance with traditional styles of composition. References to Lord's work often appear in biblical scholarship concerned with exploring the possibilities of oral composition in the Bible.[3] This is not the interest of the present study. Lord's work is of great relevance to this study, however, in that he like us deals with traditional literature, its characteristics and forms, literature which reflects a cultural and literary tradition wider than the individual composer who is its product. The "singer of tales" belongs to a tradition of storytelling in

[2] Albert B. Lord, *The Singer of Tales* (New York: Atheneum, 1968); David E. Bynum, *The Daemon in the Wood: A Study in Oral Narrative Patterns* (Cambridge: Center for Study of Oral Literature, 1978).

[3] See, for example, Robert Culley, *Studies in the Structure of Hebrew Narrative* (Philadelphia: Fortress, 1976) 20–25; *Oral Formulaic Language in the Biblical Psalms* (Toronto: University of Toronto, 1967).

which certain ways to express ideas and images and to choose
and put together the pieces of a tale become as natural, even as
typological, as the patterns of speech in his native language.
Lord is interested in the nature of narrative structures, showing
that works such as the *Odyssey* and the *Iliad* are composed of
chains of traditional patterns of content, "themes," which themselves are composed of smaller pieces of content, "motifs."[4] His
approach is an implicit form of structuralism, one with interesting synchronic, comparativist, and diachronic dimensions having great relevance for the present study of the narrative
themes of Genesis 1–11.

First comes an examination of each thematic whole of
Genesis 1–11, removed from its context in Genesis. What are
the pieces of any one narrative theme and the relationships
between them? What sort of tale is created by a particular
combination of content, what are its essential meanings and
messages, and how are they conveyed by the compositional
stuff of the tale?

The synchronic study of the myths of Genesis 1–11 will
not proceed according to the order of verse and chapter now
found in Genesis. Rather, the myths will be discussed in
groupings of like material in order to highlight the repeated
patterns of content which occur in Genesis 1–11. This form of
repetition finds parallels in traditional literature, for Lord and
Bynum have shown how one composer reuses the same narrative pattern several times within a work so that it becomes
like a recurring musical theme.[5]

Intrinsic to such an examination of each narrative theme,
its pieces and patterning, is the possibility of comparing it
with comparable literature of other cultures. Lord's study of
the epic reminds us that many narrative patterns are cross-
cultural. Cross-cultural comparison is especially useful in the

---

[4] Thus, for example, *The Odyssey* contains the themes of long war, disguise,
deceptive story, recognition (*The Singer of Tales*, 97). The recognition theme
itself is made of a cluster of traditional motifs such as the initial recognizer (an
old family servant) the recognition token (the scar), and so on.

[5] A. B. Lord, *The Singer of Tales*, 84; David E. Bynum, "Themes of the Young
Hero in Serbo-Croation Oral Epic Tradition," *PMLA* 83 (1968) 1296–1303.

study of biblical myths, urging one to explore the meanings of certain kinds of narrative themes unfettered by a preconceived theology, while at the same time providing a foil for that which is unique about the biblical tradition.

After detaching the individual myths from their context in the Book of Genesis as now arranged, one will pay special attention to that very arrangement and explore the ways in which the thematic pieces of Genesis 1-11 have been combined into a compositional whole. While the examination of each theme in the earlier section is essentially ahistorical or synchronic, this examination of Genesis 1-11 is more historically oriented posing questions concerning period of composition and the authors and audiences to whom Genesis 1-11, with its recurring patterns, might have been relevant and meaningful. Bynum's work, in particular, reveals that certain basic narrative patterns have tremendous staying-power, retaining integrity over lengthy periods of time and in various traditions.[6] While undergoing transformations under the pressure of historical and cultural change, such patterns remain recognizable and relevant in the stories people tell. Awareness of the stability of certain narrative themes is of great importance in the second half of the study which moves beyond Genesis 1-11, exploring the ways in which prophetic, intertestamental, and early Christian writers employ some of the key themes uncovered in the first half of the study.

Important in this context is the boundary where the patterns of sacred texts meet the patterns of our lives as individuals and communities. The literary themes which now join to form the first eleven chapters of Genesis have had the power to reflect and affect an on-going reality. For this reason the comparative, literary-critical perspective of the study will be balanced by modes of thought found in the work of cultural anthropologists interested in uncovering and understanding the patterns of our lives, patterns expressed in various media and modes.[7]

6 *The Daemon in the Wood.*

7 Mary Douglas, *Purity and Danger* (New York: Praeger, 1969); Clifford Geertz, *The Interpretation of Cultures* (New York: Basic, 1974); Victor Turner, *The Ritual Process* (Ithaca, NY: Cornell University, 1977); *Dramas, Fields, and*

A basic human need is the need to create order, to establish categories, to differentiate like from unlike—in short, to impose a patina of orderliness on the essential untidiness of our existence.[8] We create this aura of orderliness through the marriages we contract, through the foods we eat, through the rituals we perform, and through the sacred stories we tell. Genesis 1–11 has to do with this very issue of order-making which is interwoven with the concerns about the nature of the universe and the self which began this study. One can be more specific.

Two major thematic chains emerge in Genesis 1–11 which describe two key transformations in the Israelite concept of the becoming of the universe. One involves the passage from an initial state of chaos to an ideal cosmos in which all of nature is beautifully arranged and ordered. The other involves the passage from this ideal state to reality, for the first movement from chaos to cosmos stops short of creating those social structures, hierarchies, and definitions which mark real time and the human being's everyday status in the world. These two passages emerge most clearly in the myths of Genesis 1–3, but are repeated and re-emphasized in part or in whole in the other myths of Genesis 1–11.

The notion of transformation is an important one throughout this study in marking the ground shared by the patterns of human action and the literary patterns of sacred tales. The "rite of passage," a ritual activity underlining and effecting changes in status for the members of a cultural and/or religious community, becomes, for example, a useful tool in understanding the story of Eden, its various meanings and implications.

The literary process of such a myth is no less a dynamic form than the dramatic process of ritual. Each is an expression of a quintessentially human involvement in development and change, whether that change involves the life of an individual, the growth of a community, or the earliest history of mankind.

Metaphors. Symbolic Action in Human Society (Ithaca, NY: Cornell University, 1974).

[8] The image of "untidiness" is that of Mary Douglas, *Purity and Danger*, 4.

The composer of Genesis 1–11 writes of a time which he believes to have been part of the mythic past. He recalls wistfully the existence of a cosmogonic ideal or paradise time between the initial ordering of the universe and the on-set of reality. Early Christians, however, weaving upon threads in Israelite and Jewish thought and literature, believe that the pattern of creation can happen again or, indeed, that it never ceased. Of particular fascination are the ways in which ideas of paradise emerge among writers who seek to actualize a new paradise on earth, believing themselves to be participants in a new creation. Some of these writers live in the time-frame of their myths; the terms in which these myths are formulated are adaptations of the ancient mythic themes of creation and cosmos, preserved in the first eleven chapters of Genesis.

ONE

Genesis 1–11: Five Creation Themes

Genesis 1–11: Five Creation Themes

Creation is not only the causing to be but also a process of ordering and arranging that which has become. In this sense, Genesis 1 and 2 are only two of the creation myths in chapters 1–11. The Eden events which lead to a certain order of existence are as much a part of creation as the initial unfolding of the world's topography and the formation of its inhabitants.

The Israelites, in fact, perceived different stages in the creation process, stages which are presented in Genesis 1–11 through particular literary themes. A combination of these themes is found first in Genesis 1–4 and is repeated in part or in whole three times in Genesis 1–11, each time further sensitizing the reader to the specific tempo and concerns of Israelite world-view.

As noted earlier, two major movements emerge in Genesis 1–11, the movement from chaos to order and from ideal order to reality, and each of these movements is expressed in a thematic chain. It is well at this point to outline more specifically the individual themes which compose the chains and to describe some of the ways in which they are expressed. These steps in the creation process are the framework for the first half of this study, and provide headings under which the myths will be grouped and explored. The themes outlined below are markers for later Jewish and Christian writers who seek to comprehend their place in the rhythm of the universe.

From Chaos to Order
(Gen 1:1–2:4a; Gen 2:4b-25; Gen 6:5–9:19)

Chaos: The earliest stage in the creation process and one which occupies very little space or time in the Israelite cosmology presented in Genesis 1–11. Chaos' chief characteristics are its formlessness, its homogeneity, and its timelessness. In the ancient Near East chaos finds expression in pairs of essences such as *Tōhû* and *Bōhû*, "Empty" and "Void" (see below).

Order and Paradise: A moulding of the stuff of chaos into an ideally ordered natural realm which includes the presence of mankind. It is in this stage of initial differentiation, once sea has parted from land, day from night, etc. that paradise exists.

From Ideal Order to Reality

The Emergence of Reality (Gen 3:1–24; Gen 6:1–4; Gen 11:1–9): A stage beyond the ordering of nature (the sun, the water, etc.) in which human beings emerge from paradise into a more ordinary day-to-day existence. At this point in the creation process, human status comes to involve hierarchy and various kinds of socio-structural differentiation and definition.

The Overrating or Underrating of Family Members (Gen 4:1–16; Gen 9:20–27): A shaking up of the reality established above via a challenge to normal family relationships which leads to the genealogical catalogue.

The Genealogical Catalogue (Gen 4:17–5:32; Gen 9:28–10:32; Gen 11:10–32): The underscoring of a continuous process of making categories and ordering reality through the mechanism of the genealogical list. Families of mankind are set up, their dwelling places designated, etcetera.

1

Initial Creation and Ordering

Comparative Material

In earliest times did Ymir live:
was nor sea nor sand nor salty waves,
neither earth was there nor upper heaven,
but a gaping nothing, and green things nowhere.

Was the land then lifted aloft by Bur's sons
who made Mithgarth, the matchless earth;
shown from the south the sun on dry land,
on the ground then grew the greensward soft.

From the south the sun, by the side of the moon,
heaved his right hand over heaven's rim;
the sun knew not what seat he had,
the moon knew not what might he had,
the stars knew not what stead they held.

Then gathered together the gods for counsel,
the holy hosts, and held converse;
to night and new-moon their names they gave,
the morning named, and midday also,
forenoon and evening, to order the year.

On Itha-field met the mighty gods;
shrines and temples they timbered high,
forges they formed to fashion gold,
tongs they did shape and tools they made; . . .

(Creation mythology from Scandinavia)[1]

---

[1] Excerpted from the Elder of Poetic Edda. The translation is that of Lee M. Hollander, *The Poetic Edda* (Austin: University of Texas, 1928) 3.

Before heaven and earth had taken form all was vague and amorphous. Therefore it was called the Great Beginning. The Great Beginning produced emptiness and emptiness produced the universe. The universe produced material-force which had limits. That which was clear and light drifted up to become heaven, while that which was heavy and turbid solidified to become earth. It was very easy for the pure, fine material to come together but extremely difficult for the heavy, turbid material to solidify. Therefore heaven was completed first and earth assumed shape after. The essences of heaven and earth became the yin and yang, the concentrated essences of the yin and yang became the four seasons, and the scattered essence of the four seasons became the myriad creatures of the world. After a long time the hot force of the accumulated yang produced fire and the essence of the fire force became the sun; the cold force of accumulated yin became water and the essence of the water force became the moon. The essence of the excess force of the sun and moon became the stars and planets. Heaven received the sun, moon, and stars while earth received water and soil.

When heaven and earth were joined in emptiness and all was unwrought simplicity, then without having been created, things came into being. This was the Great Oneness. All things issued from this oneness but all became different, being divided into the various species of fish, birds, and beasts. . . . (Creation mythology from China)[2]

In the beginning, nothing was here where the world now stands; there was no ground, no earth—nothing but Darkness, Water, and Cyclone. There were no people living. Only the Hactcin existed. It was a lonely place. There were no fishes, no living things.

---

[2] From the Huai-Nan Tu as presented in William T. de Bary et al., *Sources of Chinese Tradition* (New York: Columbia University, 1960) 208–9.

All the Hactcin were here from the beginning. They had the material out of which everything was created. They made the world first, the earth, the underworld, and they made the sky. They made Earth in the form of a living woman and called her Mother. They made Sky in the form of a man and called him Father. He faces downward, and the woman faces up. He is our father and the woman is our mother. *(Creation mythology of the Jicarilla Apache)*[3]

The before time, the beginning, earliest times—all is vague and amorphous, darkness, nothing. Then comes an initial ordering, definition: land from sea, male from female. Images of initial chaos differ from culture to culture as do notions of what constitutes a cosmogonic or ordering process, but the mythic pattern which traces a sequence from earliest non-order to some sort of natural order is universal, corresponding to what we have described as the first two stages in Israel's concept of the larger process of creation. The exploration of stages of chaos and order in Genesis 1–11 is best enriched by comparison with myths from cultures close geographically and conceptually to that of Israel, the Mesopotamian *Enuma elish*[4] and the Greek

[3] Excerpted from Morris E. Opler, *Myths and Tales of the Jicarilla Apache Indians* (New York: American Folklore Society, 1930) 1.

[4] The Mesopotamian creation epic which is called by its first words *enuma elish* meaning "when above" dates to the first half of the second millenium B.C., perhaps even earlier. Earliest known versions, written on clay tablets in the Akkadian language and the cuneiform script of this period, feature as protagonist Marduk, city-god of Babylon, the leading state of second millenium B.C. Mesopotamia. First millenium B.C. Assyrian versions have substituted for Marduk, Assur, the Assyrian God; pre-second millenium B.C. versions may well have existed with Enlil, city-god of Nippur, pictured as the order-bringing hero. For further reading on the *Enuma elish* see Thorkild Jacobsen's discussion in H. and H.A. Frankfort, John A. Wilson, and Thorkild Jacobsen, *Before Philosophy. The Intellectual Adventure of Ancient Man* (Baltimore: Penguin, 1971) 182–99. On Mesopotamian world-view and culture see Thorkild Jacobsen, *Toward the Image of Tammuz* (Cambridge, MA: Harvard University, 1970); Samuel Kramer, *Sumerian Mythology* (Memoirs of the American Philosophical Society 21; Philadelphia: ASP, 1944). The translation employed here is Alexander Heidel, *The Babylonian Genesis* (Chicago: University of Chicago, 1963).

Hesiod's *Theogony*.[5] Students of the literature of ancient Near Eastern tradition often refer to the literary form in which stages of chaos and order are described as a theogony and cosmogony respectively.

Genesis 1 and 2 in the Light of the
Enuma elish *and the* Theogony

The term "theogony" literally means "the creation of the gods." F. M. Cross has shown that in ancient Near Eastern accounts this theogonic portion of creation is the time when the old gods come into being and reign over chaos.[6] Indeed they are chaos. Cross has suggested that the pairs of Genesis 1, heaven/earth, empty/void may be a brief biblical hint of the ancient theogonic pairs of gods whose existence marks the beginning in the epic *Enuma elish* and the *Theogony*.

Thus in the *Enuma elish* we find Apsu and Tiamat, male and female forces of sweet water and sea (1.3–4), Lahmu and Lahamu, perhaps the silt which arises from their progenitors, the waters (1.10),[7] and Anshar and Kishar, the male aspect of the horizon, a circle which circumscribes the sky, and the female aspect of the horizon, a circle which circumscribes the earth (1.12).[8] The early verses of Hesiod's *Theogony* speak of Earth and Heaven, Erebus (Darkness) and Night, and Aether (Sky, upper atmosphere) and Day.

In any event, whether or not the biblical pairs are reminiscences of the old gods, it is certainly true that like the

---

[5] The Greek *Theogony* of Hesiod is usually dated to the late 8th century B.C. though there is substantial debate in the scholarship. (See M. L. West, *Hesiod. Theogony* (Oxford: Oxford University Press, 1966) 8, 9, 200–206 and the discussion of G. P. Edwards, *The Language of Hesiod in Its Traditional Context* (Publications of the Philosophical Society 22; [Oxford: Blackwell, 1971] 199–206). It has been suggested that Hesiod's use of creation themes is directly influenced by the creation literature of the Near East (see P. Walcot, *Hesiod and the Near East* (Cardiff: University of Wales, 1966). The edition employed is N. G. Evelyn White, LCL 57.

[6] "The Older Gods in Ancient Near Eastern Creation Myths," In F. M. Cross, P. D. Miller, and W. E. Lemke, eds., *Magnalia Dei* (New York: Doubleday, 1976) 329–38.

[7] See Thorkild Jacobsen, *Before Philosophy*, 185.

[8] Jacobsen, *Before Philosophy*, 185.

Enuma elish, the *Theogony*, and so many other cultures' creation myths, Genesis 1 and Genesis 2 tell of a progression from chaos to order, from stasis to movement and change, from timelessness to time, from formlessness to form, from a blob without man or other living things to a cosmos containing a world teaming with plant, animal, and human life. In the *Enuma elish* the passage from chaos to order is accomplished by violent confrontation between some of the old gods and their children. The static quality of the old gods, Apsu and Tiamat, the forces of the sweet and salt water respectively, is underlined by their displeasure with the noise made by the younger gods. Apsu like the *Theogony*'s Cronos seeks to destroy his own children, in this case to preserve his sleep. We should emphasize that chaos is to be understood not as disorder but as no order. Chaos is not a radical force but a conservative one, one which calls itself into action to prevent dynamic change. We emphasize this notion of theogonic chaos as found in the *Enuma elish* since it will be somewhat altered in later Jewish and Christian reinterpretations of this ancient creation pattern. Apsu is slain by Ea, the wise. Later Tiamat must be destroyed by Marduk, Ea's son. The young god splits her body into two parts out of which he makes the cosmos, the upper realm and the lower. The world comes into order with the active work of the young god: day and night are established as is the calendar; the gods are given specific functions and stations; mankind is created to serve them. Mankind, composed of the blood of the enemy god Kingu who had aided Tiamat, is to live in the full, abundant, and protected world underlined by the many names of Marduk, savior chief of the pantheon, "lord of plenty, abundance, and heavy crops" (7.65ff.). This second, ordering portion of the creation process is the cosmogony, literally, the creation of the cosmos.

The *Enuma elish* is psychologically fascinating—ultimately it is a generation gap in the family of gods that leads to a creative dynamic and the establishment of the cosmos.

One should note the sophistication of the *Enuma elish*. Not all the old gods are incapable of accepting change, for Anshar

(2.8ff.), Lahmu and Lahamu (3.4ff.) support the younger generation. Nor do all the younger gods appear to support Marduk.
As the news of Tiamat's fury is passed from Ea to Anshar, from
Anshar to Kaka, his vizier, and from Kaka to Lahmu and
Lahamu, the refrain appears, "Tiamat, our bearer, hates us . . .
Even those whom ye have created march at her side" (2.11, 14;
3.15, 18; 3.73, 76). Implicit is a message that the capacity to
change does not depend solely upon chronological place in the
geneaology of gods. Ironically, Apsu and Tiamat themselves are
responsible for initially dashing their stasis by bearing children.
Conception and birth necessarily mean change of some sort.
With the creation of earth and people, still more radical forms
of change enter with cycles of birth, life, and death. Does the
theogonic/cosmogonic process emerge differently in OT where
God is one, childless, and all-powerful?

Theogonic and cosmogonic sections can be found in Genesis
1 and 2, but the passage from chaos and stasis to order and
dynamic is telescoped. The period of chaos in Genesis 1 is
described by the rhyming terms *tōhû* and *bōhû*, by the image
of darkness on the face of the deep, and by the presence of the
spirit of the Lord hovering over the face of the water. Such is
chaos in the first Genesis account. *Tōhû* is a term of uncertain
etymology which can be deduced to mean "formlessness," "confusion," "emptiness" from the contexts of its usage in OT.[9]
Bōhû, which is always used with *tōhû*, is a parallel term meaning "emptiness" or "waste." The "deep," *tĕhôm*, is related to
Tiamat, mother goddess, the salt deep, destroyed by Marduk.
Thus the image is of void, the absence of light, non-procreative
waters, but the spirit of the Lord over it all.

The movement from this state to cosmos is accomplished
not by battle and conflict, though OT tradition preserves such
a cosmogonic battle and myth elsewhere, but by a majestic
and elegant flow of sweeping word and deed. With the word
of the Lord in verse 3 comes the creation of light and with
verse 4 the differentiating of darkness from light. The process

---

[9] On *tōhû* and *bōhû* see Manfred Görg, "*Tohû wabohû*—ein Deutungs-
vorschlag," *ZAW* 92 (1980) 431–34.

of ordering continues in the scholastic, day by day list of the author who frames the events of each day in similar language. "And God said, 'Let there be (phenomenon to be created)' and there was (the phenomenon). And God saw that the (phenomenon) was good. . . . God called the (phenomenon: name). And there was evening and there was morning the (number of) day." Day and night are distinguished, the waters above and the waters below are divided by the firmament, dry land emerges from the sea, vegetation in its many varieties comes forth, as do the heavenly lights to distinguish between day and night. The sun is assigned its place and tasks, the moon and stars theirs. On the process goes through the creation of various forms of animal life culminating in the creation of mankind in its two varieties, male and female. The careful repetition of frame language in Genesis 1, its medium of expression, is significant for its message which is one of supreme and stately orderliness, controlled change, neatness. The very texture of the language suits its meaning. God's role as protagonist is emphasized and reemphasized as is the power of his word. Note further the emphasis placed on the notion of distinguishing, dividing, specifying into species in Genesis 1. The term to divide *lehabdîl* is used in verses 4, 6, 7, 14, 18, the term for species, *mîn*, in verses 11, 12, 21, 24, 25. The repeated refrain, "It was morning, it was evening, the xth day," underlines the basic divisions of each day, units of time, which will identify the dynamic of the cosmos.

E. A. Speiser has noted that the order of creation in Genesis 1 parallels that of the *Enuma elish*. There is no doubt a shared Near Eastern notion of the way the cosmos' order unfolded. Speiser, Heidel, Frankfort, and others have drawn fine comparisons and contrasts between the biblical use of this specific pattern and that of the Mesopotamians, exploring points of contact and points of departure in religious orientation and world-view.[10] One need not go over their discussions

---

[10] Speiser, *Genesis* (Anchor Bible; Garden City, NY: Doubleday, 1964) 8–13; A. Heidel, *The Babylonian Genesis*, 82–140; H. and H. A. Frankfort, *Before Philosophy*, 236–63.

which touch upon such varied issues as ecological influences on religious belief and the nature of normative monotheism. Certain points are worth noting now, though they will be more significant in the discussion of the composition of Genesis 1–11 as a whole. First, even more than the Mesopotamian account, the Israelite myth emphasizes that cosmogony is not only a process of creation but also one of arranging, distinguishing, and ordering the natural realm. This emphasis emerges in the very fact that the period of theogonic chaos is described ever so briefly in 1:1–2. Secondly, the absence of the battle theme, with its attempted infanticide and actualized partricide, further serves to leave a picture of supreme organization, good in its very orderliness. Having Genesis 1 serve as a frontispiece for Genesis 1–11 is surely of great significance. Thirdly, subsequent myths in Genesis 1–11 will include tales of fratricide and incest, for such Freudian themes remain important in Israelite creation mythology as in the myths of other cultures; yet the initial creation account will have none of them. Humans are involved in these myths of further differentiation, not God, the creator who is changeless and timeless.

The theogonic (chaos) and cosmogonic (ordering) themes are repeated in a second creation account in 2:4–14. Much has been written about stylistic and conceptual differences between the first two accounts; scholars since the late nineteenth century treat them as the first two examples of different sources in the Pentateuch.[11] In the present analysis Gen

---

[11] For a traditional and solid discussion of sources behind 1:1–2:4a and 2:4b-3 see E. A. Speiser, *Genesis*, 3–28. For further discussion of the so-called "documentary hypothesis" as regards Genesis see his introduction, XXII-LVIII. There can be no question that the elegant, scholastic style of the first creation account differs from the folksy, proverbial style of the second. In the first, God is transcendent, creating through his words, while in the second he is anthropomorphized; he walks in the garden. While recognizing that the tale itself is much older, scholars such as Speiser believe that a 6th century B.C. author or school, a priest or priests writing in Babylonian exile, were responsible for setting down the first creation account in its current form. The second creation account is generally attributed to an epic court writer who set down this tale in the nationalistic times of the great Judaean kings (10th or 9th century B.C.). He is called "J," the Yahwist (or Jahwist in German), because he uses the name

2:4–14 is to be regarded as another side of an Israelite creation prism. How does Gen 2:4–14 specify the universal two
part pattern of chaos and ordering? The pre-time period here
is described not as watery chaos but as infertile, soggy waste.
The Lord had not yet caused it to rain on the ground so that
the grass of the field had not yet sprouted, and there was no
man to work the earth (2:5). It is interesting in this account
that the presence of mankind is considered part and parcel of
the cosmos: he, the rain, the grasses, and the earth. At this
early pre-time the Lord causes a mist to rise from the ground
and wet the land, but not yet in a fructifying way. Man is
created from the dust and filled with life. God plants the
garden with its various trees including the trees of life and of
knowledge of good and evil. Seeds in this way are sown for a
future acculturation and humanization. While this account
emphasizes division and differentiation less emphatically than
the account in Genesis 1, the description of the four rivers
and their courses do serve as geographic markers, dividers of
the cosmos into its directions and orientations. Quite visibly
the world has been ordered by these landmarks. God creates
the living creatures of "the field and the sky" and man gives
them names, thereby furthering the process of definition.
Finally a helper, a counterpart, is created for man, the woman, formed from one of man's ribs.

Gen 2:4–14 orders the natural realm, but might be described as taxonomically less self-conscious than the previous
account. The creation of animals, for example, is the fashion-
ing of "every beast of the field" and "every bird of the sky"
(2:19). No details are given of the various species. There is no
attempt to be all-inclusive. The part suffices poetically for the
whole. The author's concerns are perhaps more parochial

Yahweh, Lord, for God. Each of these sources—"P" (the priestly writer/s) and
"J"—have been traced as responsible for threads or layers of narrative throughout the first four books of the Bible.

The documentary hypothesis has been under considerable criticism in
recent years. For an excellent survey of recent approaches to the problem see
the chapter by Douglas A. Knight in Douglas A. Knight and Gene M. Tucker,
eds., *The Hebrew Bible and Its Modern Interpreters* (Chico, CA: Scholars
Press; Philadelphia: Fortress, 1984).

than those of the cosmographer of Genesis 1, Eden-bound; for
the interest of the author of Gen 2:4bff. is less in the passage
from theogonic chaos to cosmogonic order than in a third
stage, mankind's passage from a cosmogonic ideal to reality.

The Flood Narrative

The flood narrative in 6:5–9:19 is a third account in Genesis
1–11 concerned with the passage from chaos to order. It begins
with a peopled and ordered cosmos which is then covered by a
new period of watery chaos and might be called a re-creation
myth rather than a simple creation myth. Since an examination
of the theology of Genesis 1–11 awaits a re-examination of all
the myths in their current context and order in the Bible one
need not linger at this point on the reason for the flood or this
story's current relationship to 6:1–4, important though such
considerations are to a final analysis. Suffice it to say that the
flood initiates a new state of chaos. The image of return to chaos
is emphasized by 7:11 as the fountains of the deep, *těhôm*, split
forth and the windows of the heavens open, spilling forth the
waters above. In this way the waters above and below so carefully divided by the cosmogonic process again comingle, eventually covering all distinguishing geographic features such as
the hills (7:20) and killing all the living things from crawling
creatures, to birds, to beasts, to humans (7:21). The living,
changing cosmos again is rendered static, infertile, undifferentiated. That which is special about this tale of chaos and
creation is that the chaos has within it one small island of cosmogonic order, the ark. Within the ark are maintained human
beings and beasts, pairs of creatures in their species—again this
term *mîn* is used (6:20; 7:14). Food, the produce of the fertile
land, is also aboard (6:21). Only Noah and his family retain
calendrical time-consciousness, counting each day the water
falls upon the earth, noting the passage of night and day.

The ark not only represents the maintained ordering of
the natural realm with its calendar, fertility, and species. It
also maintains a state which Genesis 2–3 portrays as a step
beyond the ordering and defining of nature, the state of social

structure and culture. The ark itself is a culture-intensive structure built with man-made tools and complex prepared materials. Noah takes on the ark not only his wife and his three sons but also his son's wives. Society with its generations and marriages is maintained. Reality is suspended in the ark which bobs on the surface of pre-reality and indeed pre-creation. A cosmos floats on chaos. With the cessation of the rain a cosmogonic process takes place: the flow is closed off from the fountains of the deep and the heavenly sluices (8:2). The waters gradually recede as dry land again divides from the water (8:14). Evidence of renewed vegetation is offered by the olive leaf brought back by the dove which Noah sends forth (8:11) and finally all who are within the ark emerge to repopulate the earth (8:18–19). These kernels of nature and structure preserved in the ark, the animals and the people in their various species, descend and recreate a world. God's promise never again to strike all life by flood emphasizes the seasons into which life on earth is divided, the units of time. The process of continual and predictable renewal will never be interrupted in the same way again. The order of the cosmos is set.

> Never again for all the days of the earth
> will cease
> sowing time and harvest-time
> the cold season and the hot season
> summer and winter
> morning and night. (8:22)

The composer of the flood story himself draws attention to the similarities between the creation of Adam's world and the re-creation of Noah's. God's blessing to Noah and his sons (9:1) parallels the blessing to the first man and woman (1:28). Noah is to dominate the animal world as do the first humans (1:28; 9:2). The provision for food (9:3) echoes 1:29–30, extended by an implicit reference to 2:17. The special interdiction about the eating from the trees of life and knowledge is replaced with a more mundane custom about the way meat is to be eaten (9:3–4). With an additional injunction about murder and punishment it becomes clear that this cosmogonic myth ends firmly in a social, structured reality with its customs and even with basic law. In this respect the flood narrative differs from the creation myths in Genesis 1 and 2, which stop short of describing reality with the full accoutrements of society. The story of the emergence into reality is a separate myth and presented as a process in and of itself.

2

Tales of Emergence:
The Passage from Ideal to Reality

An Australian Tale[1]

The Southern Cross

In the very beginning when Baiame, the sky king, walked the earth, out of the red ground of ridges he made two men and a woman. When he saw that they were alive he showed them such plants as they should eat to keep life; then he went on his way.

For some time they lived on the plants he had shown them. Then came a drought, and plants grew scarce, and when one day a man killed a kangaroo rat, he and the woman ate some of its flesh; but the other man would not eat though he was famished for food, and lay as one dead.

Again and again the woman told him it was good and pressed him to eat.

Annoyed, weak as he was he rose and walked angrily away toward the sunset, while the other two still ate hungrily.

When they had finished they looked for him, found he had gone some distance and went after him. Over the sandhills, over the pebbly ridges they went, losing sight of him from time to time. When they reached the edge of the coolabah plain they saw their comrade on the other

[1] This myth is published in K. Langloh Parker, *Australian Legendary Tales* (New York: Viking, 1966) 24–25.

side, by the river. They called him to stop, but he heeded them not. On he went until he reached a huge yaraän, or white gum tree, beneath which he fell to the ground. As he lay there dead they saw beside him a black figure with two huge fiery eyes. This figure raised him into the tree and dropped him into its hollow center.

While still speeding across the plain, they heard so terrific a burst of thunder that they fell startled to the ground. When they raised themselves they gazed wondering toward the giant gum tree. They saw it being lifted from the earth and passing through the air toward the southern sky. They could not see their lost comrade, but fiery eyes gleamed from the tree. Suddenly, a raucous shrieking broke the stillness. They saw it came from two yellow-crested white cockatoos flying after the vanishing tree. Mooyi, they called them.

On went the Spirit Tree. After it flew the Mooyi, shrieking loudly to it to stop, so that they might reach their roosting place in it.

At last the tree planted itself near the Warrambool, or Milky Way, which leads to where the sky gods live. When it seemed quite still, the tree gradually disappeared from their sight. They saw only four fiery eyes shine out. Two were the eyes of Yowi, the spirit of death. The other two were the eyes of the first man to die.

The Mooyi fly after the tree, trying always to reach their roost again.

When all nature realized that the passing of this man meant that death had come into the world, there was wailing everywhere. The swamp oak trees sighed incessantly, the gum trees shed tears of blood, which crystallized into red gum.

To this day, to the tribes of that part, the Southern Cross is known as Yaraandoo, the place of the white gum tree. And the north and south points of the cross are called Mooyi, the white cockatoos.

So is the first coming of death remembered by the tribes, to whom the Southern Cross is a reminder.

This Australian myth provides a useful introduction to Gen 3:1–24; 6:1–4; and 11:1–9. It helps in establishing the morphology of a universal theme of which Gen 3:1–24; 6:1–4; and 11:1–9 are specific Israelite versions. This myth from a culture far removed from the ancient Near East opens our eyes to structural and conceptual aspects of the Genesis myths which we might have missed; we are in a sense too used to usual interpretations of them, to seeing their meaning and message solely in an Israelite, Yahwistic, or at least an ancient Near Eastern context.

The inclusion of various myths of chaos and ordering sensitized us to the pattern of (1) formlessness, indistinction, non-differentiation; (2) emergence of discriminated features of the cosmos, a natural order of animals, vegetables, and minerals, a recognizable universe. This myth introduces a second thematic chain which has to do with a second stage in the differentiation process which is creation: (1) cosmos in which there is no society, no social structure, no clear definition of what it is to be human, a paradise of sorts; (2) event which disturbs the state of equanimity; (3) establishment of reality with socio-structural roles, society, and a clear definition of humanness.

The Australian myth like the biblical myth in Genesis 2–3 begins at the time of origins, "the very beginning," when Baiame, the sky king, walks the earth as does Yahweh in the garden before the revelation of Adam and Eve's disobedience (3:8). Baiame makes the first human beings, two men and a woman, out of the red ground. Like Yahweh, Baiame shows the humans the plants which will serve as their food, though in contrast to the biblical account there is no interdiction about what not to eat. There is an assumption of vegetarianism; there are no normal marriage conditions. In the Australian account the irregular marriage situation is emphasized by the odd man out arrangement of those created; there are two men and one woman. Conditions before and after the coming of reality emerge in the Australian myth as follows:

nature	*culture*
food is vegetable, that which grows and regenerates on the land, that which is there to be gathered	food is meat, that which must be acquired by hunting and killing—a culture-intensive activity
no death	death
two men and one woman, a non-marriageable set	one man and one woman, a marriageable couple

The change from the beginning state to a cultural state which is to be reality's norm is initiated by an event in nature itself, a drought which causes plant life to die. The drought begins an irreversible process of change. To survive, one man kills a kangaroo rat which he and the woman eat. The killing of the kangaroo rat and the eating of it transform an ideal early pre-reality into reality. The natural becomes cultural, as a man acts for the first time as a cultural being killing another living creature in order to eat and survive. Humans consume the kangaroo rat and by doing so make that which had not been food into food. They breach an unspoken sort of territoriality and by doing so rearrange the relationships between all beings. Ironically, a human must bring death into the world to prevent his own death. The aborigine tale has an additional significant twist. One of the two first men refuses to eat the meat, holding on in a sense to the old world and the old relationships. He dies and is raised to the divine realm, his eyes to become stars in the Southern Cross. Thus for the first time a human dies. His death makes possible a normal male/female cultural couple and begins a world in which humans can belong to the divine realm only by dying.

The theme of this tale is the emergence into reality; the tale deals with the human's becoming a cultural being whose life-setting is reality. The most salient feature of the human condition before this emergence is non-differentiation. In the Australian myth, before the drought, the human is simply one of the other living beings on earth, and peacefully co-exists with them. Death has no place in his meaning scheme and in some sense, at least in his own consciousness, he is indistinguishable from Baiame, his creator. At the same time he is part of the earth, made of it, sustained by its produce. After the drought and the hunt, humans are defined, beings clearly set apart from animals, gods, and earth; the human is the hunter and animal-eater; he is the talking, thinking being who dies; he is distinguished from and alienated from the red ground which can no longer sustain him. The emphasis on a passage from a state of non-differentiation to a state of clear differentiation is even stronger in Genesis 2–3, the first of our biblical tales of emergence.

What is fascinating about the juxtaposition of the first two creation accounts with the Eden story in chapter 3 is that in contrast, for example, to the *Enuma elish*, the world-creating events which precede the story of Adam and Eve do not lead to the setting down of reality. Granted, the natural realm in its goodness is ordered and set—sea is divided from dry land, salt water from fresh, the sun shines by day, the moon by night, and so on; yet in terms of human interaction, in terms of social structure, the world is in a state of pre-reality. This pre-reality is paradise. Whereas in the *Enuma elish* mankind is set on earth with a specific function and state of being, in the beginning as it is now, the Genesis account pauses to relate a tale of how humans reached their present state, of how their reality came about, and by doing so to emphasize that once things were easier and better. In this way, like comparable myths of so many cultures, Gen 2:4b-3 provides comfort in two ways: It explains why we are in our present human condition; such explanations allow us better to accept the pains which this condition entails. Secondly, and most important for continuing Israelite, Jewish, and Christian traditions, it provides an image of an ideal time for which one can strive, to which one can hope to return, for the door to Eden is not closed eternally once man and woman emerge from the garden—at least as far as the continuing tradition is concerned.

Genesis 2:4b-3

If one reconstructs conditions in Eden before "the fall" one finds a lack of emphasis on certain categories and statuses which become extremely important in the reality which follows: The man does not obtain food by hard work. Genesis 1:29 and 2:16 indicate that God places the vegetation before his human creations for sustenance. Genesis 2:5 and 2:15 identify the man as a tiller of the soil, but his work ethic before eating the forbidden fruit contrasts sharply with the notion of eating b'ṣbwn, "by pain all the days of your life" (3:17). Thus man, the laborer and provider, is a category of social structure not yet fully articulated. Similarly, as noted by the anthropologist Edmund Leach, there is no procreation in the garden.[2] Genesis 2:24 is a nice proverbial aside in which the composer momentarily stops his plot to comment on the marriage bond. Eve's role as mother does not begin until leaving the garden (4:1) and indeed God's punishment for Eve involves that role and its pain (3:16). In Eden, Adam and Eve are described significantly as naked and not ashamed (2:25). Scholars generally point to this image as one of innocence, youth, a time of pre-concupiscence, but it is more significant than that. Clothing is a means of social definition; nakedness emphasizes our shared humanness. Man and woman moreover are naked "without shame." They have no consciousness of sexual differentiation and sexual roles before eating of the tree. It is only after the fall that Adam and Eve clothe themselves and that Adam knows Eve. Pre-reality is thus a time without key aspects of social structure as Israelites would understand and live it.[3] There is even more interesting information to be obtained from God's post-fall words in 3:14–19. Note the heavy emphasis on hierarchy found in 3:14–16.[4] The snake is to be ruled by woman and her children, and the woman

---

[2] "Genesis as Myth," 14–15.

[3] Crossan's rhetorical analysis leads him to a conclusion which touches on mine: the Eden period is characterized by "lack of differential knowledge" ("Felix Culpa," in D. Patte, ed., Genesis 2 and 3, 110). Rosenberg sees the clothing of the first couple as an indication of a "new, deadly stance of opposition between man and beast, as promised in 3.15" ("The Garden Story," 8).

[4] Cf. Rosenberg, "The Garden Story," 8.

to be ruled by man. In Eden the man and the woman are help-
mates (2:18), companions. Their coming from one flesh (2:23)
and their essential equality is strongly emphasized (1:27). After
the critical events of Eden, the hierarchy of social reality asserts
itself. Even the snake's changing status is fascinating in this context, for before the fall he is difficult to distinguish from
humans—he walks, he talks, indeed he thinks in a more sophis-
ticated fashion than mankind. He is certainly not subservient to
mankind. Only with the eating from the tree does he become
an ordinary, real-time snake. One other feature which charac-
terizes the Eden state concerns mortal and immortal status.
While it is certainly true that mankind is not said to live forever
in Eden, on the other hand, ironically, as long as humans do not
attempt to gain divine forbidden knowledge, the possibility for
immortality, that aspect of divinity, remains. That is, only after
the fall does God express the concern that now mankind might
grab from the tree of immortality and live forever. It is only
now that humans must be fenced off even from the potentiality.
Later images in Jewish and Christian traditions include immortality on the list of that which means paradise. In Eden, even as
described in the Genesis account, humans are in one respect less
clearly differentiated from God than after Eden.

Thus, Eden's world lacks work roles, lacks procreative
and sexual roles, lacks the hierarchial arrangements of social
structure and even certain features of the hierarchy between
animals and humans, and retains a potential for immortality.
It is in direct contrast to all included in the notion of society
and is perfectly described by that which Victor Turner refers
to as "communitas."[5]

"Communitas" and Eden

The anthropologist Victor Turner presents the concept of
communitas in connection with his studies of ritual. The concept of liminality initially defined by Arnold van Gennep is also
important in this context. Van Gennep notes that human cultures mark important transitions in life—be they changes from

5 See *The Ritual Process*, 95–97.

girl to woman, from virgin to wife, from wife to widow—by ritual passages. In traditional cultures, such rites typically are composed of three essential parts or states: (1) The separation from one's current status and role through the symbols of ritual; (2) Temporary existence as marginal or liminal being. One is in a state of "ambiguity" betwixt and between cultural statuses, no longer in one's former state, but not yet in one's new state; (3) Reintegration to the social structure by assumption of a new place in society with its obligations and rights.[6]

Turner notes that the chief characteristic of liminal persons is their ambiguity. They are "neither here nor there; they are betwixt and between the positions assigned . . . by law, custom, convention . . . " An example of such a liminal being is the neophyte in an initiation or puberty rite. He is passing from a state of childhood to adulthood. During the boundary, liminal time which comes between his former and future status the initiate is often described as possessing nothing. He may wear the disguise of a monster, wear very little or no clothing.

> As liminal beings (such neophytes) have no status, property, insignia, secular clothing indicating rank or role.[7]

Turner notes further that among themselves initiates develop extremely close ties and a spirit of egalitarism, for "secular distinctions of rank and status" have disappeared or been homogenized.[8]

From his studies of special ritual situations Turner concludes that there are two basic models for "human interrelatedness" which alternate in any culture.

> The first is of society as a structured, differentiated, and often hierarchial system of politico-legal-economic positions with many types of evaluation, separating men in terms of "more" or "less." The second which emerges recognizably in the liminal

---

[6] Arnold van Gennep, *The Rites of Passage*, (Chicago: University of Chicago, 1960).
[7] *The Ritual Process*, 95–96.
[8] *The Ritual Process*, 95–96.

period, is of society as an unstructured or rudi-
mentarily structured and relatively undifferentiated
comitatus, community.[9]

Turner's theoretical framework provides an excellent context in
which to understand the emergence into reality exemplified by
the Australian tale which began this chapter and by the biblical
myth of Eden. The analysis of the Australian myth points to
what we can now call in Turner's terms a passage from community to society. The story of Genesis 2:4b-3 presents mankind's
most significant passage as comprehended by Hebrew mythology. In contrast to ritual situations in which a movement takes
place from structure to marginality to new structure, the
human begins existence as a liminal, a marginal, passing into
the structure of reality through the events in Eden. Turner's
descriptions of liminality and the state of communitas lend tremendous insight into the true nature and meaning of the Eden
state and the contrasting state of structure which follows Eden
and places in bold relief specific motifs found in the biblical use
of the emergence theme. The following summary points to the
states of community and society, liminality and structure, non-
differentiation and differentiation which characterize Eden
and post-Eden existence.

Eden	*After the "fall"*

equality: man and woman
     woman and snake
	hierarchy: woman over
	     snake
	     man over woman

nakedness	clothedness
absence of sexual activity	procreation
man and woman without clear roles	man as tiller woman as childbearer
closeness to God: sacredness	separation from God: secularness
lack of knowledge of good and evil	knowledge

9 *The Ritual Process*, 96.

Turner provides a list contrasting structured and non-structured states as they appear during ritual passages, and it includes virtually all of the features we have noticed in the description of Eden and after-Eden.[10] Identifiers such as clothing are absent during the in-between phase; there is a lack of hierarchy and societal roles. Sexuality is not treated in normal, institutionalized, family ways. Removed from society and the mundane, liminal beings acquire a special sacred status. Adam and Eve's closeness to God, their potential for immortality, thus contrast with their condition locked out of Eden. The desire to return to this special closeness with God is one of the features which most distinguish later pinings after paradise. Finally Turner draws a contrast between "foolishness" and "sagacity" in states of non-structure and structure. As a liminal person, the passenger is removed from day to day acquired wisdom, fresh, new, uncluttered, so he can be filled with new knowledge required by his new state. In Genesis, humans come not from an old structure to a new by way of liminality and a state of communitas but begin as liminals, uncluttered of mind, "foolish," and with the gaining of knowledge all other features of their liminality disappear. They emerge from Eden, knowing, sexual, socially structured, clothed, defined, mortal beings. The passage is complete.

Process of Passage: Woman, Snake, Eating

Having established that the Eden story presents man's passage from paradise and communitas to reality and structure, we must explore the narrative more closely to establish how this transformation is accomplished.

The central characters in the loss-of-Eden event are the snake and the woman, the key action motif is the eating from God's forbidden tree of knowledge. The Lévi-Straussian notion of the mediator or intermediary is helpful in understanding the dynamic of mankind's emergence into reality.

Lévi-Strauss suggests that people perceive and describe

---

[10] *The Ritual Process*, 106. Cf. David Jobling, "Semantics," in D. Patte, ed., *Genesis 2 and 3*, 44–48.

reality in terms of oppositions or contrasts: light vs. dark; right vs. left; inside vs. outside; nature vs. culture. Such oppositions tend to emphasize the discords within us and around us. The symbols of our myths and rituals help to resolve tensions implicit in the pairs even while acknowledging their contrariety. They do so by providing third items which partake of both sides of the oppositions. Thus the divisive pair becomes a unifying triad. Balance is achieved in a symbolic system which creates a wonderful image of wholeness and stability. Lévi-Strauss refers to the in-between item as an intermediary, the bridging of the oppositions as mediation.[11] For example, the mediating qualities of a Moses or a Jesus are essential to believers who face the chasm between the divine and the human. Such men, above others in their special closeness to God, partake of the divine and yet they remain human. The snake, the woman, and the eating in a sense partake of both sides of our Eden/Post-Eden oppositions and thereby provide the stepping-stone or doorway from Eden to reality. The most important opposition in understanding these mediators is that between sacredness or God-closeness and profanity or earth-boundness. To understand the role of the snake or serpent one must look more widely into his place in ancient Near Eastern myth.

One important characteristic of the serpent emerges in the ancient Near Eastern classic, *The Gilgamesh Epic*, a work to which we will return later. The serpent steals the plant of immortality given to the hero Gilgamesh by Utnapishtim, a Noah-like but immortal survivor of a great flood. The snake who sloughs his skin at regular intervals was believed to be endowed with the quality of immortality—he thus partakes of one side of our sacred-human dichotomy.[12] On the other hand,

---

[11] For an introduction to Lévi-Strauss' concept of the intermediary see his *Structural Anthropology* (New York: Doubleday, 1967) 202–27; *The Raw and the Cooked: Introduction to a Science of Mythology* (New York: Harper & Row, 1970); Edmund Leach, *Claude Lévi-Strauss* (Harmondsworth, Middlesex, England: Penguin, 1976).

[12] See the detailed discussion of the snake as symbol of immortality in Mesopotamia and Egypt in Karen Randolphe Joines, "The Serpent in Gen 3," *ZAW* 87 (1975) 1–3.

as emphasized by the declarations following the act of disobedience, he is in many ways the lowliest and earthiest of
creatures. He crawls on the ground, not lifted above it by the
faintest of legs; he is said to eat dust. He is literally sustained by
earth, a part of it. The snake is thus a betwixt and between
creature, one appropriate for linking paradise and reality. The
snake as portrayed in Genesis 3 has one further ambiguous
dimension that underscores the irony of the Eden event.

The snake in his wisdom before the fall is peculiarly divine
and human. It is man's knowledge after the fall, his ability to
think independently and differentiate good from evil, which
most makes him fully human, which distinguishes him from the
other creatures on earth, but it is also this knowledge which
makes him like a divinity. God himself acknowledges the
divine component of man's newly found wisdom when he
expells him from the garden. "Behold man has become like one
of us knowing good and evil . . ." (3:22). The Rabbis later in the
tradition also acknowledge that man's ability to distinguish is
one of his heavenly attributes (*Gen.Rab.* 8:11). Before the
events of Eden, however, it is only the snake among the garden
creatures who exhibits the special human-divine quality which
is the knowledge of discrimination. The reason he offers for
God's interdiction concerning the tree (3:5) parallels God's own
admission at 3:22. No wonder the Rabbis suggest that he is cog-
nizant of the exaggeration in Eve's notion that she cannot even
touch the tree. He is clever; he is the trickster; he is at once the
most human and divine earthly creature in the garden. Thus,
once again, he is the perfect intermediary who links the sacred,
divine, paradise realm with the human, everyday, and profane.

The woman has equally ambiguous qualities in Hebrew
thought which qualify her for the role of intermediary.
Woman's child-bearing capacity marks her with human and
divine qualities, the sacred and the profane both being implicit
in her procreative and incubative roles. She houses the mysterious process by which living beings are produced, but those
whom she brings forth are little humans, earthly creatures who
return to dust. Her monthly menstruation and the discharge
following child-bearing are polluting, even chthonic, and at the

same time dangerous, separating, and sacred. The biblical laws on women's purity testify to an ambiguous attitude to women in Israelite world-view. It is no coincidence that she is implicated in the process whereby initial life is transformed into reality.

The breaching of God's territoriality, the eating from his tree, is the supreme act of mediation, for humans literally consume that which is of God and forbidden and thereby become more like him. It is the irony of the biblical myth that man and woman become fully human, consigned to a world of status, social structure, differentiation, and strong role definition when they fail to respect the separateness of the divine. One must become divine to become human; by reaching for the ultimately divine realm from one's limbo in Eden one thrusts oneself into reality, further away from divinity. Yet is this passage not inevitable?

It has been an interest of writers from Augustine to C. S. Lewis to speculate on what things would have been like had Adam and Eve obeyed. The Rabbis note that had man not the evil inclination which causes Eve and Adam to go against God's command that no one would marry, build houses, or engage in commerce. The evil inclination was in some sense necessary to get the world rolling. What is the point of view of the author of Genesis 2:4b-3? Disappointment and disapproval are expressed by God: *mah zō't 'āsît*, "What is this you have done?" The snake, Adam, and Eve are meted out punishments which of course correspond to their roles and existence in reality. Yet there is no heavy emphasis in Genesis 2–3 on sin, on evil entering the world, or the like. Man must work with difficulty upon an often unyielding land, woman must bear children with pain, but the essential goodness of the world has not been altered. Genesis 2–3 provides a wistful model of what might have been, but the reality presented is not all inherently evil or depressing. It is reality—and indeed this reality is dynamic with birth and death, growth and decline. The ideal stasis of Eden had delayed the full implementation of the creation and ordering of the world.

Two More Tales of Emergence in Genesis

The pattern—ideal, mediation of divine and human categories, emergence into reality—expresses an essential Israelite understanding of the unfolding of the cosmos. This pattern is found twice more in Genesis 1–11, once in an abbreviated myth in 6:1–4 which is now juxtaposed with the story of the flood, and once in the Israelite version of the myth about the variety of human languages in 11:1–9.

Gen 6:1–4 opens with a description of an early time: "It was when mankind began to multiply on the face of the earth and daughters were born to them. . . ." In this brief line, no "communitas" hints are found to parallel those of Genesis 2–3; yet the narrative which continues unmistakably traces a passage from ideal to reality via divine-human interaction. The sons of God see that the daughters of men are comely and choose for themselves wives among them. Thus a sexual bond furnishes a graphic form of mediation between the divine realm and the human. Instead of the humans' eating from God's tree, the divine beings initiate sexual communion with mankind's offspring. Immediately comes verse 3 in which a limitation is set on human lifespan. The act of mediation once again ironically leads to reality and to an emphasis on mankind's earthly status. The absorption of the divine makes mankind not more divine but more human. Verse 4 presents some problems of interpretation. The text states either that giants were on earth in the early days when gods intermingled with women and that these giants were warrior heroes of old, or that the offspring of the gods and women were warrior heroes of old. Note the ambiguities in pronouns:

> And the giants were on earth in those days (and also afterward) when the sons of god came to the daughters of men and they (the daughters) bore to them. They were the strong men who from days of old were men of renown.

In any event two things are worth emphasizing. First, this myth is absolutely devoid of negative value judgement. Certainly as Genesis now stands, the story in 6:1–4 is juxtaposed with the story of the flood via verse 5, a line laden with value judgements. It is this whole, the sons-of-god myth plus the flood myth, which becomes the central concern of the post-biblical tradition of the Book of Enoch to be discussed in chapter 5. Yet 6:1–4 stands on its own, a schematic snippet of an older and no doubt richer mythic tradition which reveals the unmistakable pattern of a passage from pre-reality to reality. It is a brief reminiscence of an emergence theme. A second interesting point is that while Genesis 2–3 is set in mythic time, the earliest of mankind's days on earth, Gen 6:1–4 is set in a somewhat later early time—perhaps one might call it heroic time. Thus the opening image is not of absolute communitas—there is procreation for example—but the limitation on life-span introduced in verse 3 clearly indicates that this myth tells of a pre-real time, an ideal which the association of divine and human moves closer to real time, one of the most basic features of which is death.

Gen 11:1–9 presents a third version of the pattern, ideal/mediation/reality. The opening situation in Genesis 11 emphasizes the homogenous quality of the early time in a beautifully graphic way: All people speak the same language. The mediation between God and humans leading from unity to diversity, from non-differentiation to clear differentiation, this time is vertically spatial, the building of a tower to the heavens. The reaction of God to his divine council (Gen 11:6) echoes the fears of Gen 3:22, but more specifically emphasizes the power of communitas. With the diversification of languages comes the safer human condition in which no one understands his neighbor, in which people live scattered on the face of the earth. Supermen cease and reality, the essence of which is stratification and diversity, asserts itself. The passage from ideal to reality is even more marked in a Sumerian version of this myth in which pre-reality is described thus:

> Once upon a time there was no snake, there was no
> scorpion,
> There was no hyena, there was no lion,
> There was no wild (?) dog, no wolf,

There was no fear, no terror.
Man had no rival.
In those days, the lands Subur (and) Hamazi,
Harmony-tongued (?) Sumer, the great land of the
    decrees of princeship.
Uri, the land having all that is appropriate (?),
The land Martu, resting in security,
The whole universe, the people in unison (?),
To Enlil in one tongue . . . [13]

Security, harmony, the absence of fear, all being provided on
the land, unison—these are the characteristics of the cosmogonic ideal, communitas, paradise before the emergence into
reality. The "Tower of Babel" narrative in Genesis again contains no negative theological value judgement when read as a
complete myth in itself. Ironically, because they act to avoid
being scattered over the face of the earth (11:4), people are in
fact scattered. The divine ones are portrayed as fearful of
humans and their potential, when mankind is a whole without
the divisions of language and territory, for indeed such a pre-
emerged being is more than a mere human. The tales of emergence provide comfort not only in that they explain why we are
as we are today, societies of socio-structurally defined and differentiated, finite humans but also in that they declare that our
earliest ancestors lived as something more than mere humans in
terms of environment, lifespan, goals, and potentials.

Another Near Eastern Example

The Epic of Gilgamesh provides a fascinating example of
the pattern of emergence into reality, further enriching our
study of the biblical accounts. This epic, composed in the
fertile crescent ca. 2000 B.C., deals with the adventures of two
heroes, Gilgamesh, king of Uruk, a city-state of southern Babylonia, and his alterego and intimate friend, Enkidu. In The
Epic of Gilgamesh, the ideal-to-reality pattern is not found in
an independent creation story but is employed to describe the

---

[13] Text taken from Samuel Kramer, "The 'Babel of Tongues': A Sumerian Version," JAOS 88 (1968) 108–11.

genesis and development of Enkidu. Enkidu undergoes a personal rite of passage which parallels those of mankind in the three biblical examples discussed above. His transformation provides one of the important leitmotifs of the epic which itself deals with such basic human issues as the inevitability of death, the relationship between the individual and society, and the acceptance of responsibility.

When first created by the gods as a companion and counterpart for Gilgamesh, Enkidu belongs to the realm of the wild animals. Indeed he is not differentiated from them; he is a part of nature. His body is covered with hair (1.2.36); he knows nothing about people or land—about culture (1.2.38);

> With the gazelles he eats grass;
> With the game he presses on to the drinking-place;
> With the animals his heart delights at the water.
> (1.2.39-41)[14]

Enkidu overturns the traps of the hunter, turning back the incursions of culture into his realm.

Enkidu's transformation into a socialized man, his passage from nature to culture, is accomplished by a sexual encounter with a courtesan, sent to him by Gilgamesh for that express purpose of socialization. After they have relations, Enkidu loses his animal strength (1.4.27-28); the animals flee from him (1.4.24-25), for he has become a man. "But he had intelligence, wide was his understanding" (1.4.29). Enkidu is initiated into the realm of the human, the social, the knowing. The courtesan teaches him to "drink strong drink, the fixed custom of the land" (2.3.14). Enkidu eats bread, anoints himself with oil, and put on clothing (2.3.15, 24-27). Now Enkidu, a man, attacks the wild animals and protects the shepherds from them. His transformation is complete.[15]

It is no coincidence that Enkidu's rite of passage is

[14] Translation employed is that of A. Heidel, *The Gilgamesh and Old Testament Parallels* (Chicago: University of Chicago, 1975).
[15] Cf. the comments of G. S. Kirk, *Myth. Its Meaning and Functions in Ancient and Other Cultures* (Berkeley/Los Angeles: University of California: 1973) 148-52 and those of Joel Rosenberg, "The Garden Story," 7. Both emphasize nature-culture dichotomies in Enkidu's transformation.

accomplished by sexual relations. As in Gen 6:1-4, it is an ideal symbolization of the transformation of beings and worlds, an ideal symbolization of movement and change. Enkidu the wildman comes to absorb the courtesan's humanness, her culturalness, and is transformed into something new. Moreover, as is implicit in Genesis 2-3, sexual consciousness and the mating of human beings is one of the aspects of our existence which most make us social beings, beings in distinct sociostructural relationships with one other. Once Enkidu has such a relationship, even a temporary one, he is socialized; he has participated in society on a basic level. In the Genesis account of the events after the fall Adam's knowing Eve is further associated with the conception and birth of children. Viewed this way, Gen 4:1 emphasizes that sexual relations imply a transformation from changelessness to change, from stasis to development.[16] Mankind has emerged into a world of conception, birth, life, and death. Enkidu himself painfully learns that this too is an aspect of his existence as a human when he faces death. While the text is fragmentary at this point (Tablet 8), Enkidu appears to regret that he ever left the wild. He now realizes the full significance of what it is to be human. Humanness means change. Change means death.

Thus the author of *The Gilgamesh Epic* skillfully uses a mythic pattern of emergence to mark the odyssey of Enkidu and in the process comments on the nature of our own humanness as much as does the author of Genesis 2-3 in presenting the story of the first man and woman. We should add that the author of *The Gilgamesh Epic* like the author of Genesis 2-3, even in its current form, is not presenting an absolutely negative assessment of what it is to be human and civilized. In this we disagree with T. Jacobsen, the respected interpreter of *The Gilgamesh Epic*, as we do with many OT scholars.[17] Acknowledging that life has limits and that we are

---

[16] Joel Rosenberg ("The Garden Story," 10) suggests that the moment of "the fall" connotes a sort of "middle age" in the human life-cycle, the time between the "cessation of adolescence" and "the onset of senescence" when one first becomes aware of the transitory nature of life.

[17] Thorkild Jacobsen, *Before Philosophy*, 213-27.

finite does not necessarily mean life must be tainted or unbear-
able. Indeed this is Gilgamesh's mistake. Instead of accepting
his beloved friend's death and going on, he becomes obsessed
with finding immortality. As Siduri, barmaid who dwells by the
sea, says to Gilgamesh on his quest for eternal life:

> Thou, Gilgamesh, let thy belly be full;
> Day and night be thou merry;
> Make every day (a day of) rejoicing.
> Day and night do thou dance and play.
> Let thy raiment be clean,
> Thy head be washed, (and) thyself bathed in water.
> Cherish the little one holding thy hand,
> (And) let the wife rejoice in thy bosom,
> This is the lot of [mankind]. (10.3.6–14)

Surely Genesis offers mankind the same options for the
good life. The ideal time has passed but reality can be positive. What is interesting in fact about Genesis 2–3 is that the
passing of paradise seems quite irreversible. The on-going
tradition, however, like Gilgamesh refuses to accept this irre-
versibility and seeks the road back.

3

Shaking Up Reality and Setting It Down: Relations in the Family and Genealogies

The Underrating and Overrating of Family Members: Individualization

The story of Cain and Abel, which follows the emergence from Eden, and the encounter between Noah and his sons, which follows the emergence from the ark, play comparable roles in Genesis 1–11 and are comparable thematically, though it might not seem so at first glance. Each narrative involves an inappropriate anti-social encounter between family members, one family member's violation of the proper relationship with the other. This violation leads to the singling out of the violator and the furthering of the creation process of ordering, defining, and differentiating.[1]

Cain and Abel

Given the current arrangement of Genesis 1–11, the story of Cain's murder of Abel presents a powerful statement of world-view. The first scene depicted after the expulsion involves an act of fratricide. The reader is forced to question the goodness of the world and society as they continue to emerge. Speiser's translation of 4:7 allows for the full nominal thrust of the participle *rōbēṣ*, "the crouching one."

> Yahweh said to Cain, 'Why are you resentful, and
> why has your countenance fallen? Surely, if you

---

[1] See R. Girard's treatment of the Cain and Abel story and his discussion of incest and parricide in *Violence and the Sacred* (trans. P. Gregory; Baltimore: Johns Hopkins, 1977) 5, 74–75.

are right, it should mean exultation. But if you do
not, *sin is the demon at the door* ("The Crouching
One"), whose urge is toward you; yet you can be
his master.' (Gen 4:6–7)[2]

In this way, an early man is seen to confront a veritable per-
sonification of sin, a demon with whom he must wrestle.
Surely such an image affects the reader's view of unfolding
reality. We will return to these issues at some length when
examining the pattern and meaning of Genesis 1–11 as a
whole. First, however, we explore the pattern and possible
meanings of the myth in and of itself.

It has been suggested that Cain and Abel symbolize the
eternal battle between farmer and herdsman, between the sedentary agrarian and the semi-nomadic cattle raiser who must
travel about to find grazing for his animals. God's approval and
therefore the narrator's approval seems to belong to the herder.
In this way, the sedentary Cain's punishment, to become a wan-
derer, takes on special irony. Yet such explanations of the Cain/
Abel story tend to oversimplify at best and to allegorize at
worst. There are deeper levels of meaning in this tale of fratricide, psychological and cosmological.

Cain and Abel vie for God's approval. For an unexplained
reason God prefers Abel's sacrifice. God acts in an interesting
father role, preferring one son to the other. Cain is told he
has not "done well"; yet the reader does not know what he
has done wrong. A vegetable offering is surely as acceptable
as an animal offering. Scholars have long debated what Cain
did wrong yet one must conclude that God's preference is an
enigma.[3] It is as arbitrary as a parent's preference for the
younger child, or as unexplainable as the bird omens in the
Roman tale of Romulus and Remus in which an act of augury
does not lead to a definitive choice but to further rivalry.

In his jealousy, Cain lures Abel into the field and kills

[2] *Genesis*, 29. See also *BDB* under *ḥṭ't*.

[3] On Jewish postbiblical attempts to deal with the apparent capriciousness of
God in choosing one brother over the other see G. Vermes, "The Targumic Versions of Genesis 4:3–16," *Annual of Leeds University Oriental Society* 3 (1961/
62) 81–114.

him. Cain's curse, to wander, his expulsion from the family settlement, like Adam and Eve's expulsion from Eden, is followed by the indication that he knows his wife sexually. He forms his own family in a new location.

Cain and Abel's rivalry points to an essential tension in the family structure, a structure which is basic to the image of society and reality presented by the Genesis myths. As noted in the analysis of the flood narrative, the family and its relationships epitomize society, social structure, human order in the cosmos. All other relationships in society are extensions of the basic bonds between man and wife, parents and children, siblings and siblings. Family relationships are not static nor without tension; they can become unbalanced, broken, reformed. In one sense, in order for the process of change and development to proceed the family must be shaken up. Children must disagree with parents, establsh their own identities, leave home and found families; brothers must part to form their own families and so on. Generation gaps and sibling rivalries are, in fact, essential to the realization of an identity apart from one's family; otherwise one does not develop. The ancient creation myths see the very unfolding of the cosmos in terms of these family tensions and breaks and indeed present the most violent acting out of the tensions, aggressions, and rivalries. In the *Enuma elish*, Apsu, the father, would kill his own children in order to retain the quiet of his stasis; his children do kill him as well as their progenitress, Tiamat. It is from the parents' carcasses that the world is formed. The passing of power from the old static generation to the younger doers thus happens in the most violent and definite forms which human imagination can conjure. The family is collapsed, confused, and confounded in order that a new sort of structure be formed.

Genesis contains numerous examples of sibling rivalries of which the Cain and Abel story is the most violent and the most mythological. Esau's rivalry with Jacob, the latter's trickery, and the former's subsequent desire to kill him lead to the separation of the two brothers and in the OT history to the formation of two nations. Joseph's rivalry with his brothers and the brothers' would-be fratricide become important links in the formation of north-south divisions in Israel's tribal history. The story of Cain and Abel story so similar in many ways to the Roman foundation myth is the earliest and most extreme biblical example of this pattern: rivalry in family; violent separation; new family, structure, ordering.

One might describe the motif pattern or theme as "underrating of relatives[4]/individualization," i.e., the underrating of a relative leads to the differentiating of the violator or underrator from his former family. What is interesting to the student of biblical and other traditional literature is how this same essential pattern can be specified and particularized in varying genres and narrative contexts. In the *Enuma elish*, the "underrating" theme becomes the narrative link which achieves the passage from chaos/theogony to initial order/cosmogony. In the stories about Jacob and Joseph, this theme is part of larger cycles of stories about biblical heroes and is a step in the course of the younger brother's eventual success. In Genesis 1–11, the theme becomes a separate myth in and of itself, marking a stage in the defining and ordering of mankind. This theme is thus a vehicle of differentiation in both cultures, but the Israelite composer of Genesis 1–11 does not conceive of Yahweh as a parent-killer or child-killer; he is one and all-powerful, without progenitors, without family. Instead, the family-confrontation mode of making order becomes a matter between humans. Humans effect separation and definition via fratricide. This use of the theme is necessitated by the theology of the writer, but in turn becomes a particularly effective comment on the specific nature of reality and the challenge of being human.

The pattern we call "underrating/individualization" is not unique to the ancient Near East anymore than the emergence pattern discussed above. The way in which the pattern is specified in the Cain and Abel story might best be compared with the Roman myth of Romulus and Remus. If we further magnify the basic motif pattern of the underrating theme—rivalry

---

[4] The terms "underrating" and "overrating" in reference to parricide/infanticide and incest are commonly used by Lévi-Strauss. See, for example, *Structural Anthropology*, 211–12.

in family/violent separation/new family structure—the following comparison emerges. We are employing Livy's version (*History of Rome* 1.6.3–1.7.3).[5]

Cain and Abel	Romulus and Remus
1. Heroes are two brothers, offering sacrifice	1. Heroes are two brothers, founding a city.
2. Rivalry: whose sacrifice is more pleasing to God.	2. Rivalary: who should give city its new name and rule over it.
3. God chooses Abel.	4. Attempt to calm down or resolve explosive situation: allow the gods to choose by augury.
4. Attempt to calm down or resolve explosive situation: Yahweh's words to Cain at Gen 4:6–7.	3. Remus sees six vultures while Romulus sees twice that many: the gods have chosen Romulus.
5. Cain kills Abel in anger.	5. Bloodshed results among followers of each brother and Remus is killed in the fray.
	(Variant:
	2. Remus intensifies rivalry by mocking Romulus: he leaps over the walls of the city-to-be.
	5. Romulus kills him in anger.)
6. Cain is forced to become a wanderer, but founds a city, furthers civilization. He is differentiated from his brother and separated from his family but as an individual founds his own line.	6. Romulus becomes sole power of the city to be called by the name of its founder; Roman civilization begins.

There are some interesting variations in the use of the pattern and its motifs. Note the order reversal in steps 3 and 4 above. Also, in the biblical account, it is the favored son who is killed in jealousy; in Livy's account, the favored son or his followers do the killing. Plutarch notes that some say that Romulus feigned his positive omen; in this version of the story Remus would be both chosen and killed.[6] In any event, both Cain and Romulus react to a rejection of sorts; Cain is

[5] LCL, Livy, Books I and II.
[6] LCL, Plutarch, *Lives*, Romulus 9.4–11.3.

rejected by God, Romulus is rejected by his mocking brother or by his brother's supporters. The essential pattern of rivalry between brothers/violent separation by death/emergence of new societal configuration/furthering of civilization is quite alike in biblical and Roman accounts.

This underrating theme takes on specifically Israelite theological coloration because of the role of sin in the biblical account, because of God's warning to Cain, and finally because of God's punishment of and curse against Cain. In the biblical version fratricide is murder. This holds great significance for the view of creation and reality in Genesis 1–11 as a whole. In the *Enuma elish* and the Romulus-Remus narrative from Livy the parricide/fratricide is not presented with the same negative value judgement. Such are the events of mythic or heroic times.[7] Nevertheless, the foundation-myth quality, the on-going unrolling of reality is still very apparent in the Cain and Abel narrative, for the underrating theme interlocks with the next theme, the genealogy.

Noah and His Sons

While one aspect of family tension emphasized by cosmogonic myths involves the severe underrating of a relative, aggressive resentment which often ends in violent death (parricide, infanticide, fratricide), another aspect of unbalancing the family structure involves the extreme overrating of a relative, incest. Incest would seem to be the reverse side of the rivalry/separation pattern noted above. Instead of establishing one's identity by separating oneself from relatives or violently separating them from oneself, one alters family structure and family relationships in new and socially unacceptable configurations whereby children become spouses or parents become spouses. Freud has shown that Oedipal urges, however subconscious and sublimated, are as much a part of human development as the often more overtly expressed

---

[7] Horace, however, suggests that Rome's problems with civil war stem from these tainted origins (*Epod* 7.17–20), and Ovid (*Fasti* 4.809ff.) attempts to soften the fratricidal theme by having a compatriate of Romulus, Celer, kill Remus (see R. M. Ogilvie, *A Commentary on Livy*, Books 1–5 (Oxford: Clarendon, 1965) 54.

competitions, resentments, and rivalries. Again, the myth-makers employ incest overtly in narrative patterns and show the overrating of relatives to be another potential route of change, development, and restructuring, another possible means whereby the cosmogonic process continues.

Thus a strange narrative about Noah and his three sons appears after the emergence from the ark (9:20–27). Noah, here pictured as the first tiller of the soil, a vinter, drinks his wine and becomes drunk. His son Ham "sees his father's nakedness" and tells his brothers who do not look but take special pains walking backward to cover their father's naked-ness. The text emphasizes that they do not see Noah's naked-ness. Upon awakening, Noah knows what his youngest son has done and curses Canaan, the son of Ham, saying he will be a slave to Shem and Japheth. This text is intriguing and diffi-cult. First we note the confusion between Ham and Canaan. Noah's errant son is Ham; yet it is one of Ham's sons (10:6) who is cursed. The preserver of this tale clearly uses it for polemical purposes, to justify the Israelites' conquest of and dominance over the Canaanites and indeed to insult a cul-tural rival and political enemy. Thus the descendants of Ham/Canaan are to be cursed, the slaves of the descendants of Shem and Japheth. It is from Shem that Abraham is descended.

So much for the historicization of the myth. Yet a major question remains. What exactly does Ham do to his father? What is this scene in 9:22 really about?

> And Ham, father of Canaan, saw the nakedness (way-yar' . . . 'et 'erwat) of his father and told his two broth-ers outside.

On one level Ham appears to be insulting the old man by gaz-ing upon him when he is vulnerable and naked in a drunken stupor. He furthers the insult by sharing it with his brothers. Understood in this way, the tale evokes those of Marduk and Zeus in which there is a generation gap between the inactive, impotent senex and the active, alert youth able to challenge the old one's power and to flaunt his or her decadence to other youths. Yet the language used in verse 22 has definite sexual overtones as well.

The word 'erwâ, nakedness, is used in a variety of idioms which refer to sexual activity. The most common, employed throughout the incest taboos of Leviticus 18, is "to reveal or uncover the nakedness of . . . ," lĕgalōt 'erwat, as in Leviticus 18:15. "The nakedness of your daughter-in-law do not uncover. She is your son's wife. Do not uncover her naked-ness." This phrase does not simply mean that one is not to take off the clothes of such a person, but rather is a clear euphemism for sexual intercourse. The phrase used in Genesis 9 is not "to uncover the nakedness of" but "to see the naked-ness of." Are the implications the same? The "seeing" phrase is found in Leviticus 20:17 where it appears to be parallel to the "uncovering" phrase.

> If a man takes his sister, the daughter of his father or the daughter of his mother, and sees her nakedness and she sees his nakedness it is a shameful thing and they will be cut off before the eyes of their nation. The nakedness of his sister he uncovered. His sin he shall bear.

Taking, seeing, and uncovering seem to be synonymous in this prohibition.

The phrase "to see the nakedness" is also used in Lamen-tations 1:8 and Ezekiel 16:37 where the sinful Jerusalem is personified as an adulteress. The powerful image in Ezekiel 16:37 may well mean that God, the husband, gives the unfaithful wife over to her former lovers for their sexual abuse. Then Jerusalem will face the humiliating judgement imposed upon the suspected adulteress (16:38).

> Therefore I will gather all your lovers upon whom you took pleasure, all whom you loved and all whom you hated, and I will gather them against you from all sides and I will uncover your nakedness to them and they will see all your nakedness. (37)

> And I will judge you with the judgement of adulteresses

and blood-spillers and will set upon you the blood of anger and jealousy. (38)

One seems well justified, therefore, in suggesting that Ham's actions have strong sexual overtones. He sees his father's nakedness; his brothers do not see, but "cover up the nakedness of their father" (9:23) and reverse his actions. The fact that Shem and Japheth are said to walk backwards avoiding the sight of their father does seem to indicate that some sort of literal seeing or avoidance of seeing is involved in 9:20ff. One need not suggest that Ham actually has intercourse with his father; yet the seeing of his nakedness is itself a sexual act, an act of sexual control, an act of incest (cf. Lev 20:17).

The incestuous character of Ham's action having been suggested, questions remain about the mythological function of this brief narrative and its relevance to our earlier discussion of the complementary relationship between the underrating and overrating of blood relatives.

A variant of the overrating theme appears at Gen 19:30–38 and helps to explain the function of Gen 9:20–27. Following the destruction of Sodom and Gomorrah, Lot and his two daughters dwell in a cave. To repopulate the earth (19:31), Lot's daughters decide they must lie with their father; they make him drunk, lie with him, and conceive. Their children, incestuously conceived, are the progenitors of the Moabites and Ammonites. As in the story of Noah's sons, the incest theme is a means of insulting political enemies of the Israelites. Its placement in the patriarchal narratives is somewhat uncomfortable from a story-telling point of view, for according to this narrative frame the whole world has not been destroyed; the daughters could have taken husbands from among Abraham's children, for example. Viewed out of context, the literary theme itself has clear cosmogonic, world-creating/world-ordering functions.

Lot and daughters	*Noah and sons*
"World" has been destroyed by fire	World has been destroyed by flood
A few have been spared by God who have the responsibility of repeopling the earth	same
Drunkenness of patriarch of spared family unit	same
Incestuous intercourse	Incestuous action of some sort
Significance for future ordering of the families of men: Moabites and Ammonites engendered and distinguished from Israelites.	Significance for future ordering of the families of men: Canaanites distinguished from other descendants of Noah.

There is one important difference between the way the incest or overrating theme is used in each of these examples. The incestuous act in the story of Noah and his sons is homosexual and cannot lead to a biological formation of families of men. The Lot/daughters narrative presents a more typical use of the overrating theme in a creation myth. Implicit is the notion that the world is created or aided in re-creation by the mating between relatives who normally would not mate—indeed between whom mating is expressly forbidden by the mores of the culture from whom the myth comes. Such things happened back then, in primeval time. Yet how does a homosexually incestuous symbolic action in some way further the creation and ordering process?

By overtly expressing doubly forbidden subconscious urges—homosexuality and incest—Ham breaks up his family structure in as strong a fashion as Cain who kills his brother. Ham distinguishes himself, however notoriously, from the other brothers as much as Cain does from his. By acting moreover in a sexually dominant way towards his father, Ham asserts himself over the old man as much as do Zeus and Marduk in more violent ways over their progenitors. Thus the overt overrating of a father can shake up the structure of the family as much as the violent underrating of a brother. It can be no coincidence that the incident in Gen 9:20ff. is followed by a genealogy explaining the continuing process of diffusion and ordering of mankind just as the Cain event is followed by its genealogy.

Genealogy: Gen 4:17–5:32;[8] 10; 11:10–32

The genealogy is not characterized by a narrative pattern of motifs as are the other themes of Genesis 1–11.[9] Nevertheless, the genealogy is a literary entity distinguished by a recognizable combination of certain expected pieces of content: The naming of lines of descent (in 4:17–5:32; 10; and 11:10–31); the indication of length of time members of the line live (in 5;11:10–31); the indication of where certain members settle (in 4:17–25; 10; 11:10–31); the indication of the activities of certain members, e.g. work-roles, city foundings (in 4:17–25; 10).

The genealogy serves to highlight the continuing ordering of the cosmos. Thus Cain's separation from his family is followed by his founding a line of descendants whose culture-bringing characteristics mark the further defining of reality. Among these descendants are Jabal, "the father of those who dwell in tents and have cattle" (4:20), Jubal, "the father of those who play the lyre and pipe" (4:21), and Tubal-Cain, "the forger of all instruments of bronze and iron" (4:22). In this way, Adam's descendants through Cain found key aspects of man's life on earth as a cultural being; the living in artificial man-made dwellings; the domestication of animals; the composition of music; and the working of the earth's minerals into usable products.

The very outlining of who begets whom and how long certain ancestors live (chapter 5) underlines the world-ordering aspect of the creation process. So too the lines of descent outlined in the genealogy of chapter 10 and the more detailed

---

8 In the structure of Genesis 1–11, the genealogical material in 4:17–5:32 provides one theme. One should note, however, that behind this theme as now constituted are at least two separate genealogical sets or sources. 4:17–26 is generally attributed to the epic writer "J" and most of chapter 5 to the 6th century B.C. "P." See Speiser, Genesis, 34–43.

9 For an excellent study of the biblical genealogy in cross-cultural perspective, see Robert R. Wilson, Genealogy and History in the Biblical World (New Haven: Yale University, 1977).

information in chapter 10 about Nimrod's "mighty hunter" status, about his travels and the cities he builds. Chapter 10 is concerned with the earth's divisions into territories, peoples, and languages. Its boundary-drawing should be viewed in a larger world-ordering context. The same applies to the lines of descent and the periodizations of lifespans in the genealogy of chapter 11. It is significant that each of these genealogies closes a chain of creation/ordering themes which appears in part or in whole three times in Genesis 1–11.

TWO

Genesis 1–11: The Re-creation of Themes

4
Genesis 1–11 as a Whole

In exploring comparatively the thematic structures of each of the tales of creation and ordering, repeated patterns have emerged which have allowed us to group individual narrative pieces of Genesis 1–11 under the thematic headings: chaos/theogony; order/paradise/cosmogony; establishment of/emergence into reality; overrating/underrating of relatives; genealogy. We have also noted that these themes are links or building-blocks of larger chains. We may now explore the way these chains come together to form the structure of Genesis 1–11 as a whole. To what thematic and theological ends have the individual myths been presented, combined, and composed in this particular form? What sort of composer should we expect to have been responsible for preserving Genesis 1–11 in this way?

Structure

Genesis 1–11 exhibits a clear structure of repeated patterns. The following outline shows the thoughtful way in which an author has arranged the myths of Genesis 1–11.

I.	A. Gen 1:1.2:4a	Chaos to Ideal Order
	Gen 2:4b–25	Chaos to Ideal Order
	B. Genesis 3	Ideal Order to Reality
	C. Gen 4:1–16	Underrating of relatives (shake-up of family structure)
	D. Gen 4:17–5:32	Genealogy (further definition)
II.	B. Gen 6:1–4	Ideal Order to Reality
	A′. Gen 6:5–9:19	Chaos to Reality

	C. Gen 9:20–27	Overrating of relatives (shake-up of family structure)
	D. Gen 9:28–10:32	Genealogy (further definition)
III.	B. Gen 11:1–9	Ideal Order to Reality
	D. Gen 11:10–32	Genealogy (further definition)

While the above structure does not display a perfect chiasm or the like, it does show repeated patterns of concern, reinforced notions of how the world first unfurled. The passages from chaos to order and from ideal to reality are especially prominent, but equally interesting in sections I and II is the role of a temporary collapse of expected structure, via fratricide or incest, which leads to a further defining of the roles and relationships of human beings on earth. The genealogy which ends each of the sections as defined is part and parcel of the ordering of the universe. Such are the messages of these repeated patterns if one takes each myth individually; yet there are combined messages as well. That is, if one reads Genesis 1–11 in order from first creation to last genealogy, one must conclude that the world was created and recreated, that the process was on-going. The inclusion of three sets of genealogies further emphasizes the continuing nature of the world-creating process. There are various transformations, all of which lead eventually to reality. How does the composer view this reality? Is there a steady development which he traces from Genesis 1–11 or at least certain repeated refrains?

Progressions in Genesis 1–11: Implicit Point of View

The very placement and arrangement of the myths of creation, emergence, and fratricide in Genesis 1–4 create important messages. In a second combination, the tale of emergence in 6:1–4 precedes the tale of renewed chaos and creation through flood; the flood myth is then associated with the tale of Ham's anti-social behavior. The second set reinforces and indeed furthers the messages of the first set in chapters 1–4. Reading Genesis 1–11 in order and as a whole, one cannot but conclude that a good and bounteous earth contains a creature, the human, who has the potential by his choices to make life on that earth less good. The fall itself it not as theologically depressing an event as the juxtaposition of the expulsion from Eden with the first murder, the murder of a brother at that. The coming of reality thus not merely marks the loss of an ideal, a "communitas," but in the view of the composer of Genesis 1–11 also the beginning of a violently competitive and aggressive existence in which brother is pitted against brother. The inclusion of Lamech's war cry at 4:23–24 furthers this impression. This interesting and difficult snippet of ancient poetry remains a mystery to scholars:

> Lamech said to his wives:
> Adah and Zillah, hear my voice;
> wives of Lamech, pay attention to what I say,
> I have killed a man for wounding me,
> a young man for striking me.
> If Cain is avenged sevenfold,
> Lamech seventy-sevenfold.

This piece, written in the parallel style of Hebrew poetry, appears to be a war-cry or warrior's boast.[1] Its origins, probably tribal, are impossible to ascertain. Perhaps it once concluded a narrative piece which is now lost. In its current location in Genesis, however, preserved among the genealogical information of 4:17ff., it contributes to a larger, building message about the nature of mankind. This warrior's boast was placed here by the composer of Genesis 1–11 not merely as a scholastic act of archival preservation but because it echoes the themes of murder and vengeance which have become, in his view, a part of human culture.[2]

The juxtaposition of an ancient myth about the coming of reality with the story of God's destruction of the world furthers this negative impression. While, as noted above, Gen

[1] On the literary form of Gen 4:23–24 see Otto Eissfeldt, *The Old Testament: An Introduction* (Oxford: Blackwell, 1965) 66.

[2] Robert R. Wilson suggests in a somewhat similar vein that the inclusion of Lamech's cry in the genealogy at 4:17ff. contributes to "the Yahwist's account of man's increasing sin" (*Genealogy and History*, 155).

6:1–4 itself is absolutely free of negative value judgement—
the mating of divine and human beings leads to a limit on
life but such is reality—this myth is taken by the composer of
Genesis 1–11 to be as significant theologically as the fall, an
event even more dangerous in mankind's mythic past. We
have no way of knowing if a fuller version of the tale in Gen
6:1–4 existed at the time of the composition of 1–11. In any
event, God's reaction presented in verses 5–8 gives a definite
slant to the image of the reality which has emerged through
the descent of the sons of God: (1) the wickedness of mankind
is great; (2) human beings think only to do evil; thus not only
their actions but their internal thoughts, inner motivations,
and wishes are directed evilly; (3) God is sorry he ever
created the living creatures of the cosmos; (4) he wishes to
destroy all people but the good Noah. This reaction is much
more radical than any which follows Eden. Mankind has
reached a nadir and God decides that the creation was a big
mistake. He must try again with Noah and his seed.

We have noted that the chaos-to-creation process in the
flood account does not lead to a new paradise ideal and communitas. Again, in the overall arrangement of Genesis 1–11 this
becomes important. Upon emerging from the ark, mankind has
the stabilizing benefit of the family structure but also, significantly, laws about the eating of blood and bloodshed (9:4–6).
After Lamech's cry and the Cain and Abel incident, this emergence into reality is given more boundaries. Moreover, God's
relationship with mankind is somewhat more formalized and
structured by the covenantal promise to Noah never again to
destroy all flesh by flood (9:8–17), while Noah relates to God via
sacrificial ritual. Yet even this newly ordered reality is crashed
by the action of Ham, Noah's son, leading to the father's curs-
ing his own son. The recreated cosmos is never to be truly
orderly. New rules clearly will be needed.

While the final myth in Genesis 1–11, the tower narrative, does not continue the progressive decline of mankind
into a reality which seems less and less good, its placement is
an appropriate final comment on the state of mankind point-
ing back to problems presented by the thematic clusters,

"Creation-Eden-Cain" and "Descent-Noah-Ham." Reality is to involve dissonance, difference, lack of community between people, and a separation from God.

Such is the image of creation one receives if one reads Genesis 1–11 as a linear tale cycle with a consistent theology, a continuous narrative in which each transitionary comment is significant, in which the combination of tales is extremely important. Our individual reading of the myths revealed profound truths about the nature of creation, the process whereby creation became an initially ordered cosmos and the cosmos reality. This second reading, however, shows how a composer has taken creation material which itself has a point of view about the goodness of the world and the inevitability of reality, about the dialectic of order and reordering, and presented it and arranged it in such a way that it becomes a reflection on disobedience and sin, disapproval and separation, paradise lost. This subtle change in the material is achieved by certain key transitions such as 6:5–8, by certain nuances in the way stories are presented (see above on Gen 4:7), but primarily by presenting the material as a history, a progression whereby each tale rests upon the comments on the last. Thus, instead of having three myths about chaos, creation, and order (Gen 1:1–2:4a, 2:4b–25, 6:5–9:19), three myths about the coming of reality (Gen 3, 6:1–4, 11:1–9), two tales about overturned family structure that leads to further differentiation, (Gen 4:1–16; 9:20–27), and three genealogies (Gen 4:17–5:32; 9:28–10:32; 11:10–32)— repeated patterns which reemphasize the notion of creation as ordering—one has a linear progression which traces a pattern of increasing violence and repeated disobedience and which presents civilization as separation of humans from one another and of humans from God.

This periodization or historicization of various myths, some of which are variants of the same essential pattern, is an important occurrence in the history of biblical narrative. The very genre of the individual myths is changed when they are blended together into one narrative which leads from Adam to Abraham, for myths as myths do not fit into simple linear time-frames. The second creation account in Genesis, for example, is another perspective on the cosmogonic process, another side of the same prism; yet set up as these two accounts are in Genesis 1–11, one is led to questions about how this second creation alters the first. Similarly, the story of Cain and Abel can be compared with the founder's myth of Romulus and Remus; yet placed in Genesis 4 after the events of Eden it becomes a comment on the *direction* of the cosmos and mankind, not merely a statement about their natures. The flood story minus the introduction in 6:5–8 is a good creation myth, one which points to cycles of chaos and order in the universe. Yet when the flood is placed after previous creations and emergence myths and motivated by man's progressive sinfulness, a sinfulness somehow caught up in the very notion of real time having come about (6:1–4), a direction is set of progressive decline. The impression of cycles of chaos and order recedes as a more linear progression asserts itself.

An important contributor to this linearization is the author's use of genealogies. While each genealogy serves in its own context to underscore the continuous defining and differentiating of the universe, each is also the potential stuff of history. Generation by generation, the genealogies emphasize the diachronic, through-time quality of history as one character dies and another is born. We do not mean to evoke the incorrect generalization that myths are timeless and changeless. The myths of creation and world-ordering connote transformation, the passage from chaotic stasis to active, youthful change being one of the most important. The myths of many cultures trace a progression from early dream-time to real time, recalling the days when gods walked the earth. Myths themselves do have time sequences: Marduk is born after Ea, Ea after Anu, etc. Genesis 1–11, however, takes many myths which are in essential ways synchronic repetitions and sets them up diachronically as if one similar mythic event followed another. The genealogies help in this process, and the final result is an interestingly historical rendition of mythology.

Finally, then, we must ask who put together this historical mythology. Are identifiable viewpoints and concerns apparent? What is unique about this particular presentation of creation and ordering myths which in many ways are so similar to those of other cultures?

The majority of scholars suggest that Genesis 1–11 was set in its current form by the "Priestly Codifier." The Priestly Codifier is the name assigned by scholars to the hypothesized sixth century B.C. person or group believed responsible for much of the collecting, editing, and redacting of the literature in the first four books of the Hebrew Scriptures. The activity of the Priestly Codifier, often referred to as "P," is posited to have taken placed in Babylonian exile; "P" comes from among the religious intelligentsia and the cultic leaders of Jerusalem exiled to Babylonia by the conquering Babylonians in 587 B.C. Clearest evidence of such priestly activity is found in Numbers and Leviticus where ritual and sacral materials are preserved. Such material would have been of special concern to the Jerusalem priests, but "P"'s activity is suggested to be traceable throughout the Tetrateuch.[3]

Scholars have disagreed about the so-called "P" source, some viewing it as a continuous narrative strand running from Genesis through Numbers,[4] others emphasizing that "P" was not a narrator but a redactor, compositor, or tradent who strung together source materials.[5] Others suggest that greater refinement is needed in dating "P." Many priestly materials may date from before the Babylonian exile in 587 B.C. while others are exilic or post-exilic.[6] The exile lasts until 538 B.C. when the Persian king Cyrus allows exiles to return to the land. It is among this small group of returning exiles that we locate the biblical prophets Zechariah and Haggai whose attitudes reflect those of a Zion-oriented, priestly establishment.

Given the parameters of the present study, we cannot deal fully with questions concerning the identity of "P." Findings from an examination of Genesis 1–11 do, however, lead one to

---

[3] For an excellent discussion of "P" see F. M. Cross, *Canaanite Myth and Hebrew Epic* (Cambridge, MA: Harvard University, 1973) 293–325.

[4] See Ralph W. Klein, *Israel in Exile*, (Philadelphia: Fortress, 1979) 125.

[5] See F. M. Cross, *Canaanite Myth and Hebrew Epic*, 293–325.

[6] See most recently Richard E. Friedman, *The Exile and Biblical Narrative* (HSM 22; Chico, CA: Scholars, 1981).

agree that this corpus of myths, as now constituted, is at home in the thought-world of the priestly establishment of the exilic or post-exilic period, a thought-world nicely represented by the visions and oracles of Zechariah 1–8.[7] This diachronic study also leads to interesting conclusions about the nature of Genesis 1–11 which may or may not turn out to be helpful in deciding questions about a larger "P" source.

One must first take note of the self-consciously organizational, history-telling style of the mythology as presented. The particular juxtaposing of the myths is thematically significant, but the very style may teach us something about the composer. He is scholastic, anthological, a writer interested in the old myths. The very collecting, preserving, and ordering of the creation myths of Israel is part of the process of self-definition after the exile and an expression of the nationalism which follows the defeat of the Babylonians. Genesis 1–11 exemplifies the renewed interest in Israel's ancient myths one finds in other sixth century B.C. works such as Zechariah 1–8.[8]

The way in which the myths are combined in Genesis 1–11 traces a depressing pattern of increasing evil. Several of the myths portray a human situation which has become less positive (e.g. Genesis 3 [Eden]; 4:1–16 [Cain/Abel]; 6:1–4 [Descent]; 9:20–27 [Ham]). Taken individually, these tales do not cast a negative light on the nature of culture and cosmos. The cumulative effect, however, of having fratricide follow the expulsion, man's marked wickedness follow the descent of the sons of God, and incest follow the emergence from the ark is to create an image of progressive moral decline. This effect is particularly marked in the middle section of Genesis 1–11 from the descent through the flood. The juxtaposition of

[7] Note that the Zechariah 1–8 evidences the work of contributors to the tradition later than the prophet himself. See Peter R. Ackroyd "The Book of Haggai and Zechariah I-VIII," *JJS* 3 (1952) 151–56. The passages cited in our study breathe of the same spirit and represent the world-view of a particular party or group, whether the work of the prophet or of others who follow him.

[8] See Paul D. Hanson, "Zechariah 9 and the Recapitulation of an Ancient Ritual Pattern," *JBL* 92 (1973) 37–59; Susan Niditch, *The Symbolic Vision in Biblical Tradition* (HSM 30; Chico, CA: Scholars, 1980) 17–18; 73–175.

these myths implies that the emergence into reality necessarily involved man's increasing depravity, one instance of
which made him deserving of destruction.[9]

As noted by F. M. Cross, the concern with pervasive sinfulness is one of the hallmarks of Israel's exilic and post-exilic
thought, a means of explaining and understanding the trauma
of exile.[10] This concern is apparent in Zechariah's call to
repentance at 1:4–6 and more graphically in the content of
his visions: the fourth vision (3:1–10) in which the priest
Joshua is cleansed of his sin, an action symbolized by the
change in his garments from filthy to clean ones; the symbolic
scroll vision (5:1–4) in which the scroll is interpreted to be a
roving curse which seeks out thieves and perjurors; and the
symbolic vision of 5:5–11 in which the sins of the people and
wickedness itself, symbolized by a grain measure and a
woman, are imagined to be carried off from the land.[11]

The accumulated evidence from Genesis 1–11 moreover
is that human beings become increasingly alienated from one
another (Adam from Eve; Cain from Abel; Ham from Shem
and Japheth; and finally each person from each person
through the diversification of language). Again, in terms of
the creation process these myths mark and remark a normal
process of definition and differentiation, but in terms of a
progressive narrative, differentiation becomes alienation. Similarly, people become increasingly alienated from God, a
point climactically marked by the flood narrative in which
God seeks the ultimate separation from all people except
Noah and his family. The strong sense of alienation is another
important feature of exilic and post-exilic thought.

The fear of alienation from God, a crescendoing message
in Genesis 1–11, is found in the Book of Zechariah's wish-
fulfilling oracles of 2:14–17 (LXX 2:10–12) and 8:3, 7, 11,
passages which emphasize God's presence among Israel. The
hopes for unity among Israelites in difficult times of political

---

9 On "a spread-of-sin" theme in Genesis 1–11 see David J. A. Clines, *The Theme of the Pentateuch* (*JSOT* Sup. 10; Sheffield: JSOT Press, 1982) 64–73.

10 *Canaanite Myth and Hebrew Epic*, 299.

11 See Susan Niditch, *The Symbolic Vision*, 73–175.

divisiveness and social tension are expressed in images such as
Zech 3:10.[12]

Finally, the inclusion of three tales about the coming of
reality in Genesis 3; 6:1–4; and 11:1–9 reverberates the message that paradise and its state of communitas is indeed gone
forever. As one might expect, the sixth century B.C. Zechariah's hopes for a closer relationship with God and for the
removal of sin are not presented in the form of a return-to-
paradise. The best hoped for is the good life on God's bounti-
ful and essentially good earth. For Zechariah as for Haggai
this good life and the continuing relationship with God is
bound up in the practice of cult in the temple and in the
leadership of a worthy king and pure priest. The importance
of temple cult as a mediator between God and man, emphasized by Zechariah's vision of the menorah in 4:1–6a, 10b–14
and by the importance he places on the rebuilding of the
temple, also suits the world-view found in Genesis 1–11. Cult
is an activity performed by humans on earth to maintain a
relationship with the divine. The very practice of the cult
implies recognition of the distance between God and mankind which can be bridged only by special means at special
times. Moreover, temple cult as imagined in Zechariah re-
quires the clear leadership of the priest, thereby heightening
the distance between human leaders and the led. Thus Eden's
communitas is not a part of Zechariah's hopes for humanity.
For him as for the composer of Genesis 1–11, mankind must
make the best of reality.

Thus Genesis 1–11 finds its home in the thought-world of
the sixth century B.C. priestly establishment, exemplified by
the prophet Zechariah. The careful patterns of repetition
which emerge from the study of Genesis 1–11 lead one further to conclude that it is the product of an individual rather
than a group; one guiding force seems to have created this
orderly composition. The terms composer and composition,

---

12 On the social world of post-exilic Israel see Paul D. Hanson, *The Dawn of
Apocalyptic* (Philadelphia: Fortress, 1979); Morton Smith, *Palestinian Parties
and Politics that Shaped the Old Testament* (New York: Columbia University,
1971).

moreover, are to be preferred to redactor and redaction. The pieces of tradition which we have called themes have been arranged and combined with skill, imagination, wholeness of thought and of purpose. A term such as redaction does not do justice to this compositional process.

Most importantly, the examination of Genesis 1–11, the whole, has revealed how smaller pieces of the tradition gain significant nuances when combined in certain ways. As included in Genesis 1–11, the themes of chaos and creation reflect the world-view of a sixth century B.C. Israelite with a particular style and outlook. Not all Israelites of the sixth century B.C. nor of earlier centuries necessarily share the world-view reflected by Genesis 1–11, the whole. In other authors the literary themes now preserved in Genesis 1–11 evoke different responses. With this thought in mind, we set about tracing a trajectory which will reveal additional ways in which the ancient themes of chaos and creation find expression.

5

Creation Patterns in Prophetic
and Intertestamental Literature:
The Search for Paradise

The composer of Genesis 1–11, the one who shaped and blended the creation themes into their current form, preserves a history of humankind's earliest days on earth. Like his sixth century B.C. contemporaries, Zechariah and Haggai, he views reality as inevitable. Paradise is that brief time between the first ordering of nature and the establishment of ordinary, real time. The composer of Genesis 1–11 gives no reason to hope that paradise can be attained again, nor do any of the myths which he presents. In Genesis 3, 6:1–4, 11:1–9, the repeated message is that reality does come about. The paradise step is omitted from the Noah tale altogether. The cosmos which follows the renewed chaos and creation of the flood is simply a potentially good reality, not paradise. And while images of a fertile and blessed reality abound in the salvation oracles of the classical, exilic, and post-exilic prophets, most of these images are not of a cosmogonic ideal but are reminiscent of the positive reality with which Marduk provides the Mesopotamians—a full larder, peace, a fruitful and long life, all made possible in Israelite religion through the proper convenantal relationship with Yahweh. Few biblical writers hope for more than a positive reality or expect a return to paradise with its lack of hierarchy, its absolute harmony, and its de-emphasis on certain kinds of distinctions which mark human existence in real time. Yet some writers in biblical and post-biblical tradition do imagine the coming about of a new creation in which an ideal state does not inevitably and unavoidably pass into reality with its structure, hierarchy, and institutions. Among prophetic writers of this bent are the authors of Isa 11:1–9 and Isa 65:17–25. Among post-OT writers the most influential and exciting example is provided by Paul. The Pauline writings, in fact, not only evidence the "cosmogonic ideal" theme, but the larger thematic chain from theogony to cosmogony. For Paul, the creation process from chaos to paradise has begun anew; only this time paradise will not be an inevitable step en route to the emergence into reality. With Paul, the pattern of theogony and cosmogony takes on new life and meaning, but he combines traditional themes. Paul's writings evidence the most complex and in some ways complete use of the creation chain found in Genesis 1–11, but earlier writers also find portions of that chain relevant to describe their own times and their hopes for the future.

Darkness Before the Light: Chaos

OT Prophets

As one explores the writings of the OT prophets for uses of the creation themes which dominate Genesis 1–11, one finds an important thread of tradition that expects the resubmersion of the world into chaos or perceives this process as already underway. The natural realm so carefully defined and differentiated in Genesis 1, Genesis 2, and again in Genesis 9 is perceived as collapsing into disarray. For these prophets, the new chaos is a necessary step before an improved reality, a new cosmos. The creation pattern of chaos and order gains new meaning for these writers for whom reality does not appear to offer the good life.

By the time of the eighth century B.C. prophet Amos there is a well developed tradition in Israelite belief about "the day of the Lord." After the split of the kingdoms in the late tenth century B.C., Israelites never again quite experience the cultural, economic, and political heights of the imperial rule of David and Solomon. There arises the notion of a day of the Lord when God would wreak vengeance and judgement upon all of Israel's

enemies, leaving Israel again supreme in her world with attend-
ing economic, cultural, and political benefits. This concept as it
emerges in OT is closely intertwined with Near Eastern mythic
themes about the victory and enthronement of the gods and an
ancient biblical concept of holy war. We need not enter into the
subject at length here.[1] Suffice it to say that Amos points out to
his listeners that the day of the Lord is not necessarily to be a
time of victory for Israel and death to her enemies, but rather a
day of judgement for Israel itself (Amos 5:18ff.). What is fascinating for our purposes is that the judgement time involves a
shaking up of the order of the cosmos such that certain features
of that orderliness dissolve, creating a new chaos. The most
often repeated image is of the darkening of the sun, moon, and
stars, of their ceasing to function in their normal time-
demarcating way. Thus Amos 8:9 presents the image of the sun
going down at noon and the earth being darkened in the day-
time. This reversal of cosmic order is to take place "on that
day," a formula which refers to the day of ultimate judgement
(8:9). The fifth century B.C. Joel, more than any other prophet,
uses such images of renewed chaos to describe the "day of the
Lord" (2:10; 3:1–5 [LXX 2:28–32]; 4:14–16 [LXX 3:14–16]). For
him, the altering of the cosmos involves earthquakes, the darkening of the sun and moon, the withdrawal of the shining of the
stars (2:10). He also speaks of portents in the heavens and on
earth, blood and fire and columns of smoke (3:3 [LXX 2:30]).
"The sun shall be turned to darkness and the moon to blood"
(3:4 [LXX 2:31]). Thus the world experiences a form of chaos
whereby natural phenomena no longer follow their normal
course. A dissolution of the cosmos occurs before the new and
better times to follow. (See Joel 4:1ff.; Isa 13:10; also Ezek

---

[1] While S. Mowinckel set the "day of the Lord" in the context of Near Eastern
ritual (*He That Cometh* [Nashville: Abingdon, 1945] 145), G. von Rad traced origins for the tradition in the historical phenomenon of Israelite holy war, "The
Origin of the Concept of the Day of the Lord," *JSS* 4 (1958) 97–108. F. M. Cross,
however, has shown that these two options are not mutually exclusive, but complementary. See *Canaanite Myth and Hebrew Epic*, 91–111. See also A. J. Everson,
"The Days of Yahweh," *JBL* 93 (1974) 329–37.

32:2–8, in which a cluster of chaos motifs is applied to the defeat of Egypt.)

Daniel 7: History as Chaos

Scholars have long noted that Daniel 7 employs motifs of ancient Near Eastern creation myths which depict the young god's victory over chaos or sea. While earlier scholars tended to point to the Mesopotamian *Enuma elish* in which Marduk, the young god, defeats Tiamat,[2] recent scholarship finds even closer parallels in the Canaanite epic of Baal and Anat.[3] Baal defeats Yam, Sea, and is then able to build his palace. The god's building of his home is closely intertwined with world-ordering notions, for Baal's palace roof has windows to allow the waters above to enter as rain. It is no mere palace but a reflection of the very structure of the cosmos. We should also add that an important role is played in Canaanite mythology by El, father and head of the pantheon, who is depicted as a white-haired old man.

Daniel's vision in chapter 7 opens with an image of the four winds of heaven stirring up the great sea. Out of this angry, tossing sea come four beasts. The sea and the beasts evoke the time of chaos as surely as a Yam or Tiamat. Significantly these beasts are not simple recognizable creatures of the created world, but ambiguous or chaotic, dream-like combinations of features from various real animals. The appearance of the Ancient (v. 9), who can be compared to El, the destruction of the beast (v. 11), the enthronement of a younger figure (vv. 13–14) playing as it were an Israelite version of the Baal role, are elements of the world-creating pattern of ordering.

Daniel 7 is an example of a specific literary form, the symbolic vision. In this symbolic vision as in others in OT the

---

[2] H. Gunkel, *Schöpfung und Chaos in Endzeit und Urzeit* (Göttingen: Vandenhoeck & Ruprecht, 1895) 323–35; E. Heaton, *The Book of Daniel* (London: SCM, 1956) 171–75.

[3] A. Bentzen, *King and Messiah* (London: Lutterworth, 1955) 75; J. A. Emerton, "The Origin of the Son of Man Imagery," *JTS*, N.S. 9 (1958) 225–42; John J. Collins, *The Apocalyptic Vision of the Book of Daniel* (HSM 16; Missoula, MT: Scholars, 1977) 96–106.

objects seen are interpreted, thereby providing the true message of the vision, this experience of the numinous. In Daniel 7, the beasts are interpreted to mean the major kingdoms which have existed in history up to the time of the author. These kingdoms are to be destroyed and replaced with a metahistorical, everlasting kingdom belonging to the persecuted holy ones of the most high (7:25–27). Such a vision provided hope to persecuted pious Jews under the reign of the Seleucids in the second century B.C. and presents an innovative notion of chaos and creation which has not been fully appreciated by scholars. By interpreting the period of chaos with its tossing sea and ambiguous beasts to mean the passage of history, the author of Daniel 7 indicates that all of history has been a time of theogony, of chaos, awaiting the true cosmogony, i.e., the establishment of the eternal kingdom of God on earth. This is certainly a step beyond Amos or Joel in which a form of chaos descends unexpectedly to interrupt normal time and history in order to inaugurate the coming of a better reality. In Daniel 7, one is led to view ordinary normal time as chaos. And indeed by rehearsing the rise and fall of kingdoms, Daniel 7 leads one to regard all history as a kind of stasis. One kingdom replaces another—all are oppressive. What is the difference whether Babylonia leads or Persia, Persia or Greece? All will fall. If there is any process of change it traces a pattern from bad to worse. The only event on the cosmic time line which breaks through this succession of kingdoms is the divine judgement.

Daniel 7 does not speak of the nature of the new cosmos; its interest is more in the process of chaos and creation. It is an extremely significant passage for us, however, in that it shows one important way in which to regain paradise. That is, if history is chaos, soon to be followed by cosmogony, can the cosmogonic ideal of paradise be far behind?

An even stronger image of real time as chaos is found in The Book of Enoch which presents another version of the reality-bringing events of Gen 6:1–4.

1 Enoch 6–11: A Retelling of Gen 6:1–4

The narrative which concerns this study is found in chapters 6–11 of the Book of Enoch, a complex work which took form over a lengthy period. Chapters 1–11, an introduction to the book and the descent narrative, are at least as early as the second century B.C., for fragments of these chapters are among second century B.C. manuscripts of the Dead Sea Scrolls. Layers and sources have been suggested within 6–11, but we will deal with the narrative in its received form.[4]

1 Enoch 6–11 provides a detailed version of the descent-of-the-angels tale which is preserved in such fragmentary form in Gen 6:1–4. Whether 1 Enoch 6–11 is a tale inspired by Gen 6:1–4, perhaps even a commentary on it, or a reservoir of much more ancient oral literature is impossible to say. The story as presented in 1 Enoch 6–11 has a definite point of view, however, one which tallies with the message about history found in Daniel 7. The author finds the descent narrative (Gen 6:1–4) rather than the Eden narrative (Genesis 3) the most relevant or meaningful version of the emergence-into-reality theme to explain the nature of reality and the troubles of his own times. In this he contrasts, for example, with Paul.

The introductory material directly preceding the narrative in 6–11 as 1 Enoch now stands, provides an important foil for the myth of the angels' descent. In particular we refer to chapters 2–5 which emphasize the ideal orderliness of the cosmos: the luminaries of heaven follow a set orbit, the seasons pass in their expected cyclic pattern, and so on. The point of 1 Enoch 6–11 is that this orderliness has been damaged by the events described in the narrative. In contrast to Genesis 3, in which an

---

[4] 1 Enoch reflects the activities of various authors and compilers and evidences differing layers of tradition, sources, and genres. The major manuscripts are in Greek and Ethiopic; important fragments in Aramaic also have been found among the Dead Sea Scrolls. The heart of chapters 6–11 may be as early as the 3rd or possibly the 4th century B.C. See Paul D. Hanson, "Rebellion in Heaven, Azazel, and Euhemeristic Heroes in Enoch 6–11," *JBL* 96 (1977) 233 and George W. E. Nickelsburg, "Apocalyptic and Myth in 1 Enoch 6–11," *JBL* 96 (1977) 391.

The text and translation employed here is M. A. Knibb, *The Ethiopic Book of Enoch* (Oxford: Clarendon, 1978).

act of disobedience leads to reality but does not alter the orderliness of the natural realm, the disobedience in 1 Enoch 6–11
begins a process which will culminate in the dissolution of the
very cosmos.

The author of 1 Enoch employs not Genesis 3 but Gen 6:1–4
as the quintessential instance of disobedience to God. For him
the events in Gen 6:1–4 do not depict a passage from ideal to
reality but rather mark the road to reality which is a form of
renewed chaos, ultimately leading to primeval waters and the
need for re-creation. The theology of Genesis 1–11 as a whole
provides a precursor to this mode of reasoning; yet 1 Enoch
6–11 goes much further. As in Daniel 7, history, real-time, inaugurated in this case by the angels' descent, is a reign of chaos.
An important transformation of mythic themes is taking place
whereby the emergence of reality becomes synonymous with
renewed chaos; the two become intertwined in the world-view
of the author. The establishment of reality becomes not the
endpoint of a key chain of themes which corresponds to an
essential transformation in the progress of the cosmos. Rather,
the emergence of reality with its accompanying development
of culture brings man and his cosmos full circle back to chaos.
In the author's view, the pattern of creation has gone awry. The
result of the emergence into reality is a kind of moral chaos.
This reality must be destroyed so that the creation process can
proceed once again uncorrupted. The destruction of culture
and civilization must also be accompanied by an interruption of
the orderly natural realm, for the deluge is to cover all of the
trees whose varieties and characteristics are mentioned in
1 Enoch 3 and 5:1, is to interrupt the normal passage of the
seasons alluded to in 2:3 and 4, and most essentially is to make
dry land distinguishable from sea.

In the Enochic version of the descent-of-the-angels tale, the
taking of wives among the daughters of men is recognized by
the "angels, the sons of heaven" as a sin, an act of rebellion
(1 Enoch 6:3). This is a major transformation of Gen 6:1–4
which contains no such value judgement, but it is an under-
standable extension of Gen 6:5 the biblical transition to the
flood narrative discussed above. For the composer of 1 Enoch,

the descent and the deluge have a clear causal relationship. Equally interesting and significant is the way in which this composer emphasizes the culture-bringing aspects of the marriage between angels and women. In a sense, this author presents a much fuller emergence theme than does the composer of Gen 6:1–4 who preserves only the barest bones of a tale about the passage from ideal to reality. Whether Enoch evidences creative elaboration by an author or the writing down of ancient features of the tale preserved in oral tradition we cannot say. That which is clearly attributable to the author's own special world-view is the negative slant which he attributes to reality and culture. The relationship between the angels and human women is described as "promiscuous" (7:1). Moreover, the angels teach the women suspicious things, "charms and spells and the cuttings of roots and trees" (7:1). The offspring of the couples are not "mighty men, men of renown" as in Gen 6:4, but uncontrollable giants who first devour all the toil of men and then begin to devour men themselves (7:4). They are, indeed, cannibals, strange aberrations of cultural beings, beings of anti-culture. The description of 1 Enoch 7:5–7 best captures the notion of reality become chaos mentioned above: "And they began to sin against birds, and against animals, and against reptiles and against fish, and they devoured one another's flesh and drank the blood from it. Then the earth complained about the lawless ones." Note how the activities of the lawless ones affect every variety of living creature in the cosmos. The unnaturalness of the giants' activities is finally underlined by their cannibalism among themselves.

1 Enoch 8:1–4, a lengthier variant of 7:1–6, mentions one angel in particular, Azazel, who teaches humans to make instruments of war and of female beautification and ornamentation. These, too, of course, are aspects of culture, but again in the context of this narrative, they are features of "impiety and much fornication, and they went astray, and all their ways become corrupt" (8:2). "The whole earth has been ruined by the teaching of the works of Azazel" (10:8).

God's response to this corrupted world as in Genesis 6 is to order destruction by flood of all that exists except for Noah

who will father a new generation of men (10:1–3). The rebel-
lious angels, the so-called Watchers, will be bound for seventy
generations until their judgement at which time "in torment
and in prison they will be shut up for all eternity" (10:13).
The sons of the corrupt marriages will be made to destroy
themselves in battle (10:9).

1 Enoch's image of the new world to replace the old
corrupted one is rather typical of OT prophecy, and is a this-
worldly vision rather than a complete return to the communitas
of Eden. Its characteristics are long and full life, righteousness,
peace, fecundity, and sinlessness for eternity.

The author of 1 Enoch 6–11 sees his own times as a reign of
the forces of corruption and chaos, the scions of the Watchers
and the daughters of men, while he himself identifies with
Noah and his seed. For him it is only a matter of time until the
cosmogonic process completes itself, until chaos emerges into
cosmos and a better lasting reality. There is an interesting time-
warp implicit in 1 Enoch 6–11, for on the one hand it is clear
that the promised time of 10:17ff. has not yet arrived for the
author; yet on the other hand any Jewish reader of 1 Enoch
presumably would consider the Noah salvation event past. For
the author of 1 Enoch, the Noah myth is clearly alive and on-
going. All of history is telescoped as a period between the
descent of the angels and the great deluge. The author presents
history as a relatively brief time of anti-cosmos, anti-order,
which will be the first step in a whole new process of creation.

Isa 11:1–9 and Isa 66:17–25: Communitas and Return to Eden

Chaos must be followed by cosmos, ordering. A number of
the writers who view history as a new chaos expect an improved
but still rather real-time, structured new cosmos.[5] As in the
Noah account, the ideal cosmos/paradise theme which follows
the theme of renewed chaos is absent. A few biblical writers,

---

[5] One exception may be the Daniel traditions which seem to refer to the coming
of a kingdom which is mysterious in nature. See my comments in *The Symbolic
Vision in Biblical Tradition* (HSM 30; Chico, CA: Scholars, 1980) 210–12.

however, provide an alternative model for those who anticipate a new cosmos, one which does hearken back to Eden.

Date and Setting of the Two Isaianic Visions:
11:1–9 and 65:17–25

Each of these imaginings of a better future must have rendered more bearable a contemporary situation in which the author/prophet found himself. The oracles offer people who share in them promise of a world characterized by features which their present realities lack. The emphasis on a just and inspired ruler, harmony, and peace in Isa 11:1–9 suggests response to a situation of oppressive government, dissonance, possibly war. Similarly the concern with happiness, longevity, security, fecundity, and peace in 65:17–25 suggests a time of extreme insecurity and economic deprivation. Of course these constellations of difficulties characterize numerous periods in the history of Israel. That which is interesting about these two visions, in fact, is their lack of more specific historical hints or handles; they are archetypal and ahistorical in many ways and therefore have been especially reapplicable as messages of hope later in the tradition.

Each piece is currently part of a larger corpus of prophetic works. Isa 11:1–9 is among the oracles attributed to the eighth century B.C. Southern prophet Isaiah. Isa 65:17–25 is part of an interesting collection of late sixth century B.C. works which runs from Isaiah 56–66 and which probably comes from several writers of a late Isaianic school.

While scholars have debated whether 11:1–9 is a genuine oracle of the eighth century B.C. Isaiah, there are no reasons of content or style to reject it as such.[6] The general context of such a message of hope would be the troubled times resulting from the invasions, threatened and undertaken, by the eighth century B.C. Near Eastern super-power Assyria. The implication that current rulers do not rule by righteousness might apply to the reign of Ahaz (735–715 B.C.), one of the least

---

[6] So most commentaries.

popular Judahite kings who is accused of wholesale apostasy in the biblical tradition, but one cannot be more specific.

Isaiah 65:17–25 belongs to oracles written after Cyrus' decree that Jews exiled by Babylonia could return to their land (538 B.C.) and after small numbers of pioneers did return to rebuild the temple (520 B.C.) and restore, so they thought a new and purified state under God. Why then the longing after peace, etc.? As shown most recently by Paul D. Hanson and some years ago by Morton Smith, the late sixth century became a period of dashed hopes and disappointment.[7] It was a time of economic failure and political and cultural divisiveness as arguments arose between those who had never been exiled and those who returned, between rich members of the establishment and poor disenfranchised members of society, between those whom we might call religious "liberals" and "conservatives" and between political "conservatives" and "liberals." Isa 65:17–25 comes from an author who does not believe that the return from exile has brought the good life; his hopes are delayed for a future paradise.

This author's response to a particular historical situation and his use of the paradise theme imply a world-view quite different from that of his near-contemporary, the composer who included Genesis 3 in the eleven chapters which begin the Bible.

Isa 11:1–9

The first half of this oracle deals with the new Davidic king who will lead in the better time to come. Predictions about a king who will judge the poor and decide with equity for the meek of the earth do not evoke images of Eden or communitas, for a king implies hierarchy, the existence of the poor, no egalitarianism. The images in verse 6–9, however, take on new depth and meaning when understood in the light of Eden as cosmogonic ideal of non-differentiation. At first glance, verses 6–9 depict the sort of peacefulness evoked by

---

[7] *The Dawn of Apocalyptic; Palestinian Parties and Politics that Shaped the Old Testament.*

many classical and later prophetic salvation oracles. Yet when one looks more closely one notices certain interesting juxtapositions: wolves, carnivorous wild animals, will dwell with lambs, herbivorous domesticated animals—so too the leopard and the kid, the calf and the lion and the fatling. This unlikely group in turn is led by a human child. On the one hand, these are images of the unexpected, the impossible in ordinary time, which often signify apocalyptic, e.g. the deserts becoming waterways or the hills becoming plains. Having examined Eden in the light of Victor Turner's *Ritual Process*, however, one sees that the combinations of animals and finally animals and human in verse 6 imagine the breaking down of categories, categories which in real time imply aggression; for lions eat calves and wolves attack lambs. Indeed, Isa 11:6ff. goes beyond Eden in flattening out accepted categories in creation. Cows and bears feed together, their young lying together. The carnivorous lions become herbivorous like the ox. Once one comes to think of the new and better time, the paradise, in terms of non-differentiation such images are a natural extension of the creation ideal. Pecking orders and causes for aggression in the animal world are to disappear. Verse 8 has particular evocations of Eden, however. The asp and the adder, animal relatives of the serpent, are to be playmates of the human child. We recall that enmity between the serpent and the seed of the woman, mankind, was one of the aspects of post-Eden reality. This gap is now to be breached. Wholeness of the community of living beings is emphasized as the earth is filled with the knowledge of the Lord.

Isa 65:17–25

Isa 65:17–25 presents a vision of re-creation, evoking and reversing images of post-Eden reality while sharing images with Isaiah 11. The creation process happens all over again, with a new heaven and a new earth (65:17). The former things with all their previous realities and mistakes will not even be remembered; the slate is clean (65:17). That which the Lord creates will rejoice eternally (65:18). Jerusalem, now a part of the creation process, is "Joy," her people, "Exultation." Crying is to be banished. Already one senses that the pains of reality are to be softened. All will live to one hundred years; the limitation on ordinary human life while not eliminated is thus less compelling. Houses will be built and lived in, vineyards planted, their fruits enjoyed. The gratification is to be assured and immediate, "You will not build and another take up residence/You will not plant and another eat" (Isa 65:22). The emphasis on long life as well as the insistence that all one puts one's hand to will lead to fertility and fulfillment reverse the particulars and the tone of Adam's punishment in Genesis 3 which emphasizes the difficulty of man's life on the land—"In hard work you will eat all the days of your life (Gen 3:17). Thorns and thistles it (the land) will grow for you (3:18)"—and the brevity of human life— "By the sweat of your brow you will eat bread until you return to the earth, for from it I took you; for you are dust and to the dust you will return." Instead of frustration and disappointment, man "will not grow tired for nought nor bring forth (children) for dismay" (Isa 65:23). The separation between God and man which follows Eden is erased, as a wonderful communion is established between God and his people. Even before they call upon God he will respond (65:24). In verse 25 comes the communitas image seen in Isaiah 11 whereby distinctions between carnivorous beasts and domesticated animals are altered: the wolf and lamb feed together; the lion like the ox eats straw.[8]

Thus Isa 65:17–25 imagines a future in which differentiation between carnivore and herbivore is less marked, in which

---

[8] The third line in v. 25 is often regarded by scholars as an addition: "And as for the serpent, dust will be his *lehem*, 'bread/food.'" It is indeed an enigmatic phrase, one seemingly not at home in its present context. The notion of the snake's consuming bread—even dust as bread—may be a reversal of his condition after the fall, for bread-eating is a quintessentially human activity. Such an interpretation would make some sense of the phrase as it stands. On the other hand, bread, *lehem*, may simply mean food here as in other OT contexts, in which case the phrase is best omitted.

mediation between God and man again becomes immediate
and direct, in which one's work leads not to thorns but to easy
fecundity, in which sorrow is erased, life unexpectedly long—
indeed a newly created ideal in which the fears and aggressions of ordinary existence vanish (65:25). Once again, as in
Isaiah 11, the imagined future recalls Eden, but falls short of
envisioning a total reversion to communitas. The image of a
man's building his house and happily living in it, for example, is a societal image however ideal. Nevertheless, the fusing
of members of the animal world, the new closeness of the
divine and the human, the absence of aggression and fear do
point towards communitas. The communitas vision has a full
and genuine renaissance in early Christianity as revealed by
the writings of the New Testament.

6

Early Christianity:
Chaos, Cosmos, and Community

The Pauline Writings

The Pauline writings[1] offer an exciting and creative use of themes of chaos and cosmos. These writings evidence ways in which ancient mythic themes retain meaning, adapting and evolving to become a relevant expression for new socio-religious situations. In his use of themes of chaos and ideal cosmos Paul is both conservative and radical. His is a logical extension of prophetic and intertestamental uses of the images of reality-become-chaos and the return-to-Eden. At the same time, however, he weaves these images into a unified new fabric which serves to envelop the history and message of Jesus.

Chaos as Sin and Death

For Paul the chaos of reality is not merely a matter of rule by oppressive empires who make historical time out-of-joint as in Daniel 7. For him, as for the composer of 1 Enoch 6–11, chaos begins from the very instance of the emergence into reality and has to do with the very nature of mankind. While 1 Enoch regards Gen 6:1–4 as the essential tale about the coming of reality, for Paul the key piece of tradition is the account in Genesis 3. Unlike the author of 1 Enoch, who considers Noah and his seed untainted by the moral chaos

---

[1] References will be confined to Galatians, Romans, and 1 and 2 Corinthians. Unless otherwise noted, the translation employed is the RSV (2d ed., 1971).

around them, Paul views every human descended from Adam as tainted with sin, part and parcel of mankind's steady decline toward chaos. And it does seem correct to speak of a decline. For Paul, as for other writers with an apocalyptic world-view, reality has become worse and worse. It is at the worst of times, however, that one can look forward to a complete collapse of the cosmos and a new process of creation. Man's sin has been eating away at God's order until, in a sense, the support pillars give way, allowing for a fresh start.

It is in this context that we understand Rom 1:18–32. Again 1 Enoch comes to mind. The composer of 1 Enoch 1–11 contrasts the divine orderliness of the natural realm which God has created with the activities of the descendants of the sons of God and the daughters of men. So too Paul.

> Ever since the creation of the world his invisible nature, namely, his eternal power and deity, has been clearly perceived in the things that have been made. So they are without excuse; for although they knew God they did not honor him as God or give thanks to him, but they became futile in their thinking and their senseless minds were darkened (Rom 1:20–21). . . . Therefore God gave them up in the lusts of their hearts to impurity, to the dishonoring of their bodies among themselves. . . . (1:24)
>
> For this reason God gave them up to dishonorable passions. Their women exchanged natural relations for unnatural and the men likewise gave up natural relations with women and were consumed with passion for one another, men committing shameless acts with men and receiving in their own persons the due penalty for their error. (Rom 1:26–27)

The description of people's "unnatural" behavior in verses 26–27 reminds one of 1 Enoch's description of the giants' consuming one another's flesh and blood. In Paul, cannibalism is replaced by homosexuality. For Paul, homosexuality epitomizes the de-ordering of society, an instance of confusion and chaos, the collapse of culture. As early as ancient Israel the tradition exhibits tight boundaries for order and disorder which exclude homosexuality. Sexual relations between people of the same gender are treated as dangerous, order-threatening occurrences to be listed as forbidden in Leviticus 18 alongside relations with animals (vv. 22, 23).[2] Paul's contrast between "God's invisible nature . . . clearly perceived in the things that have been made" in creation and the exchange of "natural relations for unnatural" sets up an important message about cosmos and the new chaos. As in Genesis 1, the created natural realm is to be regarded as a good one, reflecting according to Paul the very power and deity of God (1:20). Chaos had been vanquished. Yet man by his activities since creation has turned the natural into the unnatural, the orderly into the disorderly and improper. As in 1 Enoch, the cosmos is perceived as crumbling under a new sort of chaos. The created boundaries of nature are breaking down because of mankind's improper conduct. This point of view contrasts with those found in the Eden narrative (Genesis 3) and the Cain and Abel narrative (Genesis 4) in which misconduct is an inevitable part of his emergence into reality, a part of the continuing unfolding of the cosmos. Paul's view is more consonant with Genesis 1–11 in its received form. Passages such as Gen 6:5–7 and 6:12 emphasize that mankind's corruption causes God to consider remaking the world, which was not supposed to turn out this way. Even in Genesis 9, however, the new start with the seed of Noah quickly falls into impropriety; that is, Ham sees his father's nakedness. We should add that while Genesis 1–11 gives in some ways a depressing view of the choices people tend to make, there is never any indication that what Adam had done effects the choices of later human beings. Each person has the opportunity to choose the good; more often than not he makes the wrong choice.

For Paul, however, Adam's wrong choice upsets in a permanent way that which had been the intended order of the

---

2 See S. Niditch, "The 'Sodomite' Theme in Judges 19–20: Family, Community, and Social Disintegration," *CBQ* 44 (1982) 365–78.

world, and unlike the composer of Genesis 1–11, Paul looks to
a time when all wrong-doing will cease, thereby restoring or
even bettering that initial intended cosmos. Romans 8:18–22,
difficult passage that it is, supports this interpretation of
Paul's world-view.[3] In this passage Paul writes of the creation
not as an action but rather as a personified entity. That which
God brought into being and ordered in Genesis 1–2, which
we have referred to as the cosmos, Paul calls the creation.
This creation in "the sufferings of the present time" (8:18) has
been in a sense suspended and now "waits with eager longing
for the revealing of the sons of God," that is, for the inaugu-
ration of the new era. Paul writes that this creation had been
"subjected to futility" (8:20), that it "will be set free from its
bondage to decay" (8:21). Verses 22 and 23 most clearly point
to the interpretation above: "We know that the whole creation has been groaning in travail together until now and not
only the creation but we ourselves. . . . " The creation or
cosmos has suffered futility, decay, travail. It awaits renewal
and reformation.

Most fascinating in Paul's view of that which the cosmos
should have been and will be again is the role played by
death.

> Therefore as sin came into the world through one man
> and death through sin and so death spread to all men
> because all men sinned. . . . (Rom 5:12)

Paul equates the time of sin with the time of death and, most
interesting of all given what we have noted above, equates
sin, death, and chaos. For Paul, the prevailing image of chaos
is not water, *tĕhôm*, *Yam*, *Tiamat*, but death, *māwet*, *Mot*.
Reality is chaos in that it is a time of sin which is death. In
this way, Paul employs an extremely ancient mythic pattern
involving the battle with death in much the same way that
OT writers employ and adapt the mythic pattern about the
victory over sea.

---

[3] For a thorough discussion of Romans 8:18–30 see Ernst Käsemann, *Commentary on Romans* (Grand Rapids: Eerdmans, 1980) 229–45.

In equating death with chaos Paul participates in a pedi-greed and ancient Near Eastern tradition. The seasonal pattern, explored so richly by Theodor Gaster in *Thespis*,[4] depicting the challenge to the young fertility god by death, his defeat and descent to the underworld, and his eventual victory over death and re-emergence is, in fact, a variant on the defeat-of-chaos creation pattern. This emerges with great clarity in the Canaan-ite Baal and Anat epic which employs both versions of the pat-tern. Baal, like the Mesopotamian Marduk, defeats Sea, Yam, and is enthroned thereby establishing his order in the cosmos. Then, however, he faces a second opponent, Death (Mot). He is defeated temporarily, eventually regaining victory with the help of his consort Anat. During his period of capture by Death, the earth becomes infertile, growth ceases, and a kind of stasis reigns; there can be no new life. With the victory over death comes restored fertility, creation—in short an active cosmos. Death's reign is as much a form of chaos as is the rule of Sea. Both imply changelessness, infertility, a pre-cosmogonic time. Generally, the chaos-as-sea motif is used in tales which depict the first creation of the cosmos and the chaos-as-death pattern in tales which refer to the cyclical interruption of the earth's growth and change, its yearly brush with the stasis of chaos in winter. Paul creatively places the death motif on the more cos-mic time-line and in this way finds a perfect medium in which to interpret the meaning of the resurrection of Jesus.

One is not suggesting simplistically that Paul borrows or is influenced by Canaanite or other Near Eastern myths. Rather such mythic patterns are a part of his way of understanding the world, a piece of the culture he shares with those whom he wishes to reach with his message. The literature of the New Testament gains new meaning when set against the background of more ancient mythic patterns as shown by Adela Yarbro Collins's excellent study of the combat theme in The Book of Revelation.[5]

---

[4] (New York: Norton, 1977).
[5] *The Combat Myth in the Book of Revelation* (*HDR* 9; Missoula, MT: Schol-ars, 1976).

Thus for Paul, the present time of sufferings is the time of death's reign. While Paul participates in an extremely ancient tradition, however, he adds to the mythic theme the additional factor of man's sinfulness. Sin caused death; death is chaos. To restore creation sin must be forgiven; then death will cease; chaos will be defeated. Paul is not the first biblical writer to associate sin with death and infertility. Such is the thrust of the theology of blessings and curses found in the book of Deuteronomy (Deuteronomy 27–28) whereby following covenant leads to abundance and fecundity, while disobedience leads to infertility, death, and sterility. This theology is found as well, for example, in the writings of the eighth century B.C. prophet, Hosea (Hosea 2). Baal worship leads to sterility and death; reintegration into a positive relationship with God means fertility and life. What is unique and so creative about Paul, however, is that he goes beyond these OT usages to form an integrated understanding of the whole pattern of creation from Adam until his own times. Death is not an intermittent punishment, but rather has impaired creation since the events of Eden. All time since then has been a reign of death, a decaying of the creation, a chaos.

For Paul, the death and resurrection of Jesus ushers in a new creation, assuredly inaugurates a new cosmos, specifically because Jesus does overcome death. This is his proof that man's sin has been forgiven by the suffering of Jesus, that the cosmos has been released from the reign of sin. If death has been overcome, sin has been forgiven.

> Then as one man's trespass led to condemnation for all men, so one man's act of righteousness leads to acquittal and life for all men. For as by one man's disobedience many were made sinners, so by one man's obedience many will be made righteous. (Rom 5:18–19)
>
> But in fact Christ has been raised from the dead, the first fruits of those who have fallen asleep. For as by a man came death, by a man has come also the resurrection of the dead. For as in Adam all die, so in Christ shall all be made alive. . . . For he must reign until he

has put all enemies under his feet. The last enemy to be destroyed is death. (1 Cor 15:20–22, 25–26)

A new creation is underway (2 Cor 5:17; Gal 6:15) and Christ is the new Adam (1 Cor 15:45). He is, however, not only the protagonist of a new Eden, but also the Baal-type warrior who defeats death, sin, chaos so that the new creation might unfold.

In this way Paul's vision of new creation goes beyond the Eden vision or makes central and explicit that which in Genesis 3 is peripheral and only implicit. That is, the cosmogonic ideal means everlasting life. As ordinary, real time means sin, death, and renewed chaos, for Paul, the new cosmic ideal is one of sinlessness, deathlessness, and perfect order all made possible by the vicarious suffering of the new Adam and confirmed by his life after death.

Nature of the New Creation:
Actualization and Communitas, A Model of the Kingdom

What is the nature of this new cosmos and human behavior within it? How is it to be reflected in the life-style of Christians who taste of the first fruits of the kingdom and in some sense attempt to actualize in the here and now the kingdom which is to come? Once again, concepts and images of Eden play an extremely important role for Paul.

For Paul, the crucifixion and resurrection of Jesus provide the doorway to paradise and the state of communitas. We have already discussed the absence of sin and death in the new reality, the overcoming of sin and death being Paul's own version of the mythic victory-over-chaos theme. The cosmos established after the victory has as one of its most salient features the lack of need for law. This cosmos is not to be governed by law. Justification by faith versus law is surely one of Paul's most difficult and complex concepts and a thorough examination of the problems associated with it will not be attempted here. However, looking at Paul's view of the law in the context of new creation, new Eden, and communitas ideal is extremely instructive.

The emergence into reality in Genesis 3 involves a passage from lack of knowledge of good and evil to knowledge of these. For Paul knowledge of evil necessarily means in some sense that we are evil. Knowing evil, one needs laws to prevent one from acting evilly; yet this only continues a vicious cycle. "Law came in, to increase the trespass" (Rom 5:20). The human being can never be completely free of sin. "I do not understand my own actions. For I do not do what I want, but I do the very thing I hate. Now if I do what I do not want, I agree that the law is good. So then is it no longer I that do it, but sin that dwells within me" (Rom 7:15–17). The law, Paul states, is not sin (Rom 7:7). It is good. But the very presence of the law and knowledge of it necessarily imply the presence of sin and knowledge of it. And people's propensity to break laws necessarily compounds and recycles their sinfulness. "Yet if it had not been for the law, I should not have known sin. I should not have known what it is to covet if the law had not said, 'You shall not covet'" (Rom 7:7).

How does Paul envision a break in this cycle of sin? All the laws in the world do not help and only provide specific opportunities to sin. Again the answer is the new creation.

> For neither circumcision counts for anything nor uncircumcision, but a new creation. (Gal 6:15)

If through Jesus, mankind returns to a state of creation's ideal, it will be again in a state of sinlessness and therefore also a state which has no need for laws governing every action.

> Now before faith came, we were confined under the law, kept under restraint until faith should be revealed. So that the law was our custodian until Christ came, that we might be justified by faith. But now that faith has come, we are no longer under a custodian; for in Christ Jesus you all are sons of God, through faith. (Gal 3:23–26)

The vicious circle is broken in a harmony of paradise. One no longer needs a law code to distinguish knowledge of good from knowledge of evil. These have no relevance in a state where knowledge really means knowledge of the Lord. If one has this essential knowledge, one need not worry about laws which distinguish proper behavior from improper, which establish property rights or inheritance rules—the earthly, mundane law fades before the spiritual law which has no such boundaries.

> The unspiritual man does not receive the gifts of the Spirit of God, for they are folly to him, and he is not able to understand them because they are spiritually discerned. The spiritual man judges all things, but is himself to be judged by no one. 'For who has known the mind of the Lord so as to instruct him?' But we have the mind of Christ. (1 Cor 2:14–16)

Indeed the disappearance of the law is a marker par excellence of the state of communitas, for the law is a creator of differentiation, pecking order, human institutions. Galatians 3:28, which continues and highlights the discussion quoted above about the end of the rule of law emphasizes the notion of communitas which is essential to Paul's understanding of the new order. "There is neither Jew nor Greek, there is neither slave nor free, there is neither male nor female; for you are all one in Christ Jesus." Paul's views on celibacy and marriage also make sense in this context, for marriage is a demarcating, societal institution differentiating family from family, setting off one couple from another. The preferred state is one of celibacy (1 Corinthians 7). Paul speaks in terms of freedom from anxiety in troubled times (1 Cor 7:27–29, 32, 40), but 1 Cor 7:29–31 is especially instructive in placing Paul's views on marriage in the larger context of the new creation which is to come:

> I mean, brethren, the appointed time has grown very short; from now on, let those who have wives live as though they had none, and those who mourn as though they were not mourning, and those who rejoice as though they were not rejoicing, and those who buy as

though they had no goods and those who deal with the
world as though they had no dealing with it. For the
form of this world is passing away.

Paul's emphasis on celibacy is not merely a matter of saving
oneself the worry of a family in troubled times or even of
being able to dedicate oneself fully to other members of the
community and to God with complete unselfishness. Rather
the very nature of reality is changing. Old categories of marriage, property, and emotions have no relevance in the new
world to come. We recall that in Eden, Adam and Eve have
no sexual relationship. There is no marriage, but the non-
differentiation of nakedness without shame. There is in Eden
no need for bought goods—all is provided.

The Pauline writings thus present a dramatic retracing
and reworking of the pattern of creation themes found and
repeated in Genesis 1–11: chaos is followed by a new cosmos
and this cosmos, like Eden, is distinguished by its state of
communitas. The ideal cosmos inaugurated by the Jesus
event, by the appearance of the new Adam, is hoped to be
eternal and not merely that theme which precedes an emergence into reality with its law, structure, and institutions.

Hints of Cosmos as Communitas in the Synoptics

The ideal cosmos with its Eden-like traits of marriageless-
ness and propertylessness also appears in other early layers of
the Christian tradition found in the Synoptics and would
seem to express a shared conception in the early Church
about the nature of kingdom to come, a conception useful to
characterize as communitas. While this study does not include
a thorough examination of the Synoptics, we point to a few
interesting passages.

Mark 12:18–27 (Matt 22:23–33; Luke 20:27–40) is a con-
troversy narrative. Thinking to make a fool of Jesus, the Sad-
ducees, who denied the existence of an afterlife, pose the
mocking puzzle:

There were seven brothers; the first took a wife and
when he died left no children and the second took her

and died leaving no children and the third likewise and the seven left no children. Last of all the woman also died. In the resurrection whose wife will she be? For the seven had her as wife.

Thus in the fulfillment of the law of the levirite or brother-in-law outlined in Deut 25:5ff., whereby the brother marries his deceased brother's childless widow to care for her and raise children in his brother's name, one woman hypothetically has been married seven times. Come the kingdom and resurrection, which brother re-assumes the role of husband to this woman?

Jesus' response underlines the concept of the new reality as a return to non-sexuality, which is non-differentiation on an important level. The institution of marriage will cease to be.

Jesus said to them, 'Is not this why you are wrong, that you know neither the scriptures nor the power of God? For when they rise from the dead, they neither marry nor are given in marriage but are like angels in heaven.' (Mark 12:24–25)

As noted in discussing Paul's view of the conquest of death, the early church goes even beyond Eden in its vision of the kingdom, as the risen are imagined to have angelic status. The otherworldly, divine quality of the state of communitas is enhanced. Yet such an emphasis on the angelic and therefore non-marriable status of those who participate in the resurrection has implications for how one lives in this time of imminence, of first fruits. We mentioned Paul's preference for celibacy. Also of note is the significant role played by women in the early church. Along with the end to marriage, an institution so important in the post-Eden state, comes an end to hierarchical orders between men and women, also a feature of post-Eden reality. Robin Scroggs, Elisabeth Schüssler-Fiorenza and others have taken stock of the leadership roles played by women in the early Church.[6] Romans 16, for

6 Robin Scroggs, "Paul and the Eschatological Woman: Revisited," *JAAR* 42 (1974) 532–37; Elisabeth Schüssler-Fiorenza, "Word, Spirit, and Power: Women

example, mentions "our sister Phoebe, a deaconness of the church at Cenchreae" (Rom 16:1) and Prisca and Aquila, presumably a married couple to whom Paul refers as his fellow-workers in Christ Jesus (16:3).

The very nature of human interaction is to change in the new reality. The institution of marriage does not belong in a realm of communitas. So too the traditional notion of the nuclear family.

> And his mother and his brothers came; and standing outside they sent to him and called him. And a crowd was sitting about him; and they said to him. 'Your mother and your brothers are outside, asking for you.' And he replied, 'Who are my mother and my brothers?' And looking around those who sat about him, he said, 'Here are my mother and my brothers! Whoever does the will of God is my brother, and sister, and mother.' (Mark 3:31–35; cf. Matt 12:46–50; Luke 8:19–21)

The normal distinctions of family status are replaced by relationships in the larger community of believers. Relationships are based on new criteria, the central one of which is to do the will of God.

Jesus' radical call to leave home, parents, and family and follow him also must be understood in this context.

> If any one comes to me and does not hate his own father and mother and wife and children and brothers and sisters, yes, and even his own life, he cannot be my disciple. (Luke 14:26)

The giving up of one's family is not merely a matter of renunciation for the greater cause or of selflessness, nor is it simply a reflection of the belief that the end-time is near so

---

in Early Christian Communities," in R. R. Ruether and Eleanor McLaughlin, eds., *Women of Spirit. Female Leadership in the Jewish and Christian Traditions* (New York: Simon and Schuster, 1979) 29–70; *In Memory of Her. A Feminist Theological Reconstruction of Christian Origins* (New York: Crossroad, 1983). Other important works include Wayne A. Meeks, "The Image of the Androgyne," *History of Religion* 13 (1974) 165–208; Stevan Davies, *The Revolt of the Widows* (Carbondale, IL: Southern Illinois University Press, 1980).

that one need not worry about building families and support-
ing them. Rather, the dissolution of the nuclear family and
the formation of a new, wider community of believers (Mark
10:29–30) is part of a complex mythology about the new age.
Christians are asked to begin to live in the style of the kingdom even before its arrival in full.

It is also in this light that the emphasis on propertylessness
must be understood. We mentioned Paul's statement in 1 Cor
7:30. Matt 6:25–34 is also relevant. G. Theissen emphasizes
the life of self-sacrifice to be borne by the outsider, the wandering follower of Jesus.[7] Yet when one looks carefully at the
passage one also sees another instance of return to Eden.
Unhampered by identifying occupations, distinctive clothing,
and status-rendering possessions, the followers of Jesus are
common-denominator members of one community. Moreover, Jesus' emphasis on "God will provide"—"consider the
lilies of the field, how they grow; they neither toil nor
spin . . ."—is not a depressing comment based on the bitter
experience of the wandering charismatic as Theisson suggests[8]
but rather another Eden hope. Before the fall, all was provided. It is only after leaving the garden that man has to
work with difficulty and often meet with agricultural failure.

> Therefore do not be anxious saying, 'What shall we eat?'
> or 'What shall we drink?' or 'What shall we wear?' For
> the Gentiles seek all these things; and your Father knows
> that you need them all. But seek first his kingdom and
> his righteousness, and all these things shall be yours as
> well. (Matt 6:31–33)

Jesus challenges his followers to adopt attitudes of Eden
as if the kingdom had already come and by doing so to help
bring it about. In this sense, the miracles of food-production
(loaves, fishes) evidence first fruits of the kingdom as much as
does Jesus' rising from the dead.

---

[7] *Sociology of Early Palestinian Christianity* (Philadelphia: Fortress, 1978),
13–14.

[8] *Sociology*, 13.

Literary Themes as a Reflection of Life

A definite picture of the promised new reality emerges from reading in Paul's letters and in selected portions of the Gospels. This picture makes sense only in the light of Eden and the return-to-paradise while expanding and building upon earlier visions in the tradition. Paul's emphasis on deathlessness, sinlessness, and the irrelevance of the law, his insistence on the non-differentiation between male and female, Jew and Gentile, and his challenge to the institution of marriage find interesting echoes in the Gospels where marriage and property are shown to be irrelevant, when family becomes the community of all believers, and where necessities such as food, drink, and clothing are regarded as natural, expected gifts of God. These characteristics moreover are not only hoped-for features of the kingdom to come but also encourage modes of behavior among Christians in the time before the coming, providing a means, in fact, of actualizing paradise on earth. It is important to emphasize that for Paul the thematic chain of chaos and cosmos reflects the real drama of mankind's history on earth. His image of the new cosmos is not merely a literary phenomenon, a reworking of ancient Eden traditions, but also a genuine expectation for the new order and a model to be followed by Christian believers. For Paul the literary themes both reflect reality and affect it.[9]

The most practical result of living in the style of the kingdom to come, in a mode which we have compared to Turner's state of communitas, has to do with the loving, brotherly relationship which should exist among these equal, sharing partners in the community. Romans 12 emphasizes the unity, love, equality, and brotherliness implicit in communitas.

> For as in one body we have many members, and all the members do not have the same function, so we, though

---

[9] Clifford Geertz's concept of "Religion as a Cultural System" is directly relevant. See his discussion of "model of/model for" on pp. 93–94.

many, are one body in Christ and individually members
one of another. (Rom 12:4–5)

Thus while each person's "gifts" and function in the community
may well differ, this does not alter the fundamental oneness of
the whole or the fact that each is part of the other.[10]

Let love be genuine; hate what is evil, hold fast to what
is good; love one another with brotherly affection; outdo
one another in showing honor. (Rom 12:9–10)

Contribute to the needs of the saints, practice hospital-
ity. (Rom 12:13)

In this way members of Christ undergo a veritable transformation in human behavior.

Do not be conformed to this world but be transformed
by the renewal of your mind, that you prove what is the
will of God, what is good and acceptable and perfect.
(Rom 12:2)

Communitas and Institutionalization:
The Re-emergence of the Emergence Theme

That which is so radical about the belief of the early
Church is the notion that the paradise ideal could be eternal
and that a transformation could occur in mankind through
Christ that would radically alter people's usual behavior, their
tendency to establish hierarchies, their jealousies, their differences. Paul challenges Christians to prove themselves altered
and capable of this state. 1 Corinthians is a fascinating record
of the difficulties associated with the attempt to live as a community, to actualize the ideal, presenting evidence of dissen-
sion, divisiveness, power-plays—in short, the very opposite of
the love attitude:

I appeal to you brethren, by the name of our Lord Jesus
Christ, that all of you agree and that there be no dissen-
sions among you, but that you be united in the same

10 See E. P. Sanders, *Paul and Palestinian Judaism* (Philadelphia: Fortress,
1977) 547.

> mind and the same judgment. For it has been reported
> to me by Chloe's people that there is quarreling among
> you, my brethren. What I mean is that each one of you
> says, 'I belong to Paul,' or 'I belong to Apollos,' or 'I
> belong to Cephas,' or 'I belong to Christ.' Is Christ
> divided? Was Paul crucified for you? Or were you bap-
> tized in the name of Paul? (1 Cor 1:10–13)
>
> . . . for you are still of the flesh. For while there is jeal-
> ousy and strife among you, are you not of the flesh and
> behaving like ordinary men? (1 Cor 3:3)

Paul preaches the communitas ideal but it is clearly not an
easy mode of behavior or attitude for all (see 1 Cor 3:8;
4:6–13). He attempts to reinforce community unity, its magic
circle about itself, by discouraging in the case of grievance
recourse to outside secular courts (1 Cor 6:1–8). The persis-
tence of the behavior pattern of the fleshy man, the man of
the old Adam's world, emerges no better than in 1 Cor
11:17–34, a passage discussed in fine detail by A. J. Malherbe
who emphasizes its socio-structural dimensions.[11] The meal
which should be the symbolic expression of Christian community becomes instead the occasion for expression of the old
fleshy self.

> When you meet together, it is not the Lord's supper that
> you eat. For in eating, each one goes ahead with his own
> meal, and one is hungry and another is drunk. What! Do
> you not have houses to eat and drink in? Or do you
> despise the Church of God and humiliate those who
> have nothing? What shall I say to you? Shall I commend
> you in this? No I will not. (1 Cor 11:20–22)

Malherbe suggests that this passage points to class problems
among Christians. The wealthy, able to bring large quantities
of food, and who, in line with Roman custom, regard priority
in partaking of the food at a banquet a sign of rank, act in a
manner appropriate to their status. They begin eating their

---

[11] *Social Aspects of Early Christianity* (Baton Rouge: Louisiana State University, 1977).

good food before the poorer participants who can eat only what the wealthy have provided them and who implicitly are expected to wait for their meal.

Those who treat the meal in this fashion fail to comprehend the sacred, "other," non-fleshy quality of this meal, fail to understand that by eating they are partaking of the body of Christ thereby uniting themselves into one body (cf. Rom 12:4, 5). Paul reminds them of the true meaning of the meal.

Inability to actualize a paradise ideal as exemplified by problems in the sacred feast is not the only challenge faced by Paul. By insisting that the new creation means the end of the rule of law, Paul actually encourages those who do not fully understand him to adopt one of the models of communitas mentioned by Turner, what we might call the libertine modality. If differences and distinctions, emphasized by the law no longer have significance, why distinguish at all?

> It is actually reported that there is immorality among you, and of a kind that is not found even among pagans; for a man is living with his father's wife. And you are arrogant! Ought you not rather to mourn? Let him who has done this be removed from among you. (1 Cor 5:1-2)
>
> Do you not know that the unrighteous will not inherit the kingdom of God? Do not be deceived; neither the immoral nor idolators, nor adulterers, nor sexual perverts, nor thieves, nor the greedy, nor drunkards, nor revilers, nor robbers will inherit the kingdom of God. And such were some of you. But you were washed, you were sanctified, you were justified in the name of the Lord Jesus Christ and in the Spirit of our God. 'All things are lawful for me,' but not all things are helpful. (1 Cor 6:9-12)

In behaving free of the law, the Corinthians are approaching the very moral chaos that preceded the new creation. Thus the actualization of an Eden ideal in the time before the parousia poses many difficulties.

There is a further dimension to consider when exploring

the Christian movement as an attempt to establish communitas. Victor Turner's work tells us that man cannot sustain communitas for very long.

> For, like the neophytes in the African circumcision lodge, or the Benedictine monks, or the members of a millenarian movement, those living in community seem to require, sooner or later, an absolute authority whether this be a religious commandment, a divinely inspired leader, or a dictator. Communitas cannot stand alone if the material and organizational needs of human beings are to be adequately met. Maximization of communitas provokes maximization of structure, which in turn produces revolutionary strivings for renewed communitas. The history of any great society provides evidence at the political level for this oscillation.[12]

To prove this point Turner briefly explores the genesis and history of the Franciscan Order, tracing a progression from Francis's own emphasis on poverty and absolute propertylessness to the eventual development of a structured organization.[13]

The same process can be observed in the Christian movement by comparing Paul's vision and the images in the Synoptics with later layers of tradition in New Testament. One superb example of this later adjustment and restructuring is found in 1 Cor 14:33b–36, a passage generally accepted as a post-Pauline addition to the letter.[14]

> As in all the churches of the saints, the women should keep silence in the churches. For they are not permitted to speak, but should be subordinate as even the law says. If there is anything they desire to know, let them ask

[12] *The Ritual Process*, 129.

[13] *The Ritual Process*, 145–47.

[14] For a careful outline of stylistic, linguistic, and conceptual reasons for regarding 1 Cor 14:33b–36 as an interpolation see Hans Conzelmann, *1 Corinthians* (trans. James W. Leitch; Philadelphia: Fortress, 1975) 246. He concludes, "In this refutation we have a reflection of the bourgeois consolidation of the church, roughly on the level of the Pastoral Epistles: it binds itself to the general custom."

their husbands at home. For it is shameful for a woman to speak in church. What! Did the word of God originate with you, or are you the only ones it has reached?

This message is a far cry from Paul's "neither male nor female" and from a church in which women such as Phoebe and Prisca play leadership roles. We note also that the subordination of women to men is justified by reference to the law (14:34), a remarkably inappropriate means of proof for one who declares the end of the rule of law. There can be no doubt that 1 Cor 14:33b–36 is post-Pauline. It breathes of a different spirit.

Communitas, the Eden state, which evens out hierarchies such as those between men and women to emphasize all persons' commonality, unity, and equality, is the ideal of the early Church, maintainable even with difficulty as long as the full establishment of God's kingdom is believed imminent. Paul expects the coming at any moment (1 Cor 15:51–52). Once this fulfillment becomes clearly delayed, man's tendency to order, to structure, to compartmentalize, to make law takes over. And indeed, while one looks back wistfully at the early Church's liberated attitude toward women, and while of course such an attitude certainly can and does work well in many branches of the institutionalized church today, certain aspects of institutionalization and structuring are necessary for a movement to survive. As Turner notes, "Communitas cannot stand alone if the material and organizational needs of human beings are to be adequately met."[15] The Church seems to have gone rather far, however, in the direction of structure and hierarchy.[16]

1 Timothy, a post-Pauline epistle dating approximately from the beginning of the second century C. E., which again most scholars agree was attributed to Paul by later tradition,

---

[15] *The Ritual Process*, 129.

[16] This movement towards institutionalization was not without opposition. The Apocryphal Acts of Paul witness to a different strand of early Christian tradition. See most recently Denis R. McDonald, *The Legend and the Apostle. The Battle for Paul in Story and Canon* (Philadelphia: Westminster, 1983).

reveals the early movement in the Church from community to society.[17] The definition of the Christian is being more clearly delineated. With definition and differentiation comes, as expected, greater emphasis on law. "Now we know that the law is good, if anyone uses it lawfully" (1 Tim 1:8).

The Church itself by now has developed a hierarchy. The office of bishop is discussed in 1 Tim 3:1ff. Again we find an emphasis on the submission of women, as the post-Eden hierarchy and roles are reasserted.

> Let a woman learn in silence with all submissiveness. I permit no woman to teach or to have authority over men; she is to keep silent. For Adam was formed first, then Eve and Adam was not deceived but the woman was deceived and became a transgressor. Yet woman will be saved through bearing children if she continues (lit. 'they continue') in faith and love and holiness with modesty. (1 Tim 2:11-15)

This passage is in its Eden reference even more revealing than the one in 1 Cor 14:33b–36. In contrast to expecting the return to the pre-fall state, so important to Paul's notion of Church community, this writer emphasizes the status quo of the post-fall state, ordinary reality. Eve's sin is recalled and presumably not swept away with faith. Implicit is the notion that reality involves Eve's submission because of her actions in the events of Eden. The woman's post-Eden role as child-bearer is re-emphasized and indeed enhanced as her means to salvation— this in stark contrast to Paul's emphasis on celibacy which, as we have shown, is intricately interwoven with notions of pre-fall paradise when people were naked and not ashamed, when no children were born. Thus if Paul seeks the doorway back to Eden, this writer reassumes the lock-out pose. "Love" as used in 1 Tim 2:15 no longer conveys the forceful notion of the communitas relationship as in 1 Corinthians, but has assumed a less technical, more watery connotation. 1 Tim 5:14 is also of

---

[17] Paul Feine, Johannes Behm, and Werner Georg Kümmel, *Introduction to the New Testament* (14th ed., Nashville: Abingdon, 1966) 258–72.

interest in this context. "So I would have younger widows marry, bear children, rule their households, and give the enemy no occasion to revile us." Young women thus are to be kept in their places as child-bearing wives. There is an uncomfortableness about the detached woman, the one not under a man's control. She has the potential to disrupt safe categories, the very sort of disruption implicit in and encouraged by the communitas ideal. The writer of 1 Timothy worries about "what the neighbors might say" of such unattached females. He wants Christians in basic features of life-style to become more indistinguishable from their non-Christian neighbors. The community has become society, a part of it.

Closing Thoughts

The pattern which leads from chaos to ideal order and from the ideal to reality has asserted itself in spite of the hopes of Paul and others for an eternal return to the middle stage of the pattern exemplified by Eden. This pattern has been seen at work in the actual life of a religious movement. The passage from an ideal state of non-differentiation to reality has been as inevitable and expected in real life as in the narrative pattern repeated three times in Genesis 1–11. One theme follows the other in a sequence which is rooted in ancient literary tradition and grounded in human experience. The communitas ideal so evident in the Pauline writings fades before the needs of an institutionalized church whose emergence begins to be evident in a work such as 1 Timothy. And yet if Turner is correct a certain degree of structure and institution was necessary if the movement was to survive.

The study of biblical creation patterns is a reminder that traditional literary themes and the ways they link together in larger chains of content do indeed reflect the way we are. The themes of ideal cosmos and emergence into reality point to a paradox within each of us and within human culture. We perceive the desirability of an eternal cosmogonic ideal which emphasizes unity, harmony, and equality. At the same time we require definition, order, differentiation to make bearable our smallness in the face of the world's enormity, to aid in the survival process of self-definition, to keep at bay the first theme found in Genesis 1–11, chaos; for chaos always threatens even once the initial ideal ordering of the cosmos has been completed. Chaos threatens in the form of uncontrollable natural forces, in uncontrollable human decisions which affect our lives, and most important in the uncontrollable sides of ourselves.

Hence Enkidu's ambivalence about the way themes of ideal order and reality have asserted themselves in his life. About to die, Enkidu at first curses the harlot who led him to knowing, socialized human status and ultimately to his death. After listening to the admonition of Shamash, however, Enkidu appears to relent. As Shamash says, the harlot had taught him "to eat bread fit for divinity, to drink wine fit for royalty," had given him a king as a friend. Enkidu's socialized status had allowed him to become a leader among men, a position he had enjoyed (7.3.35–50). Thus culture with its structures and institutions is a source of enrichment, progress, and order as well as a source of competition, aggression and, for Enkidu, death. In fact, communitas and society have a dialectical relationship. Both modes, both urges, are within us and characterize human cultures; one or the other may dominate at any one time.

Our study has shown how these dimensions are expressed and preserved in the myths of Genesis 1–11. The last chapter examines early Christianity in the light of themes of creation and chaos and emphasizes further how myths and actions in history intertwine, reflecting one another but also affecting one another. The theme of emergence into reality which is the heart of the Eden myth reflects the way real life must be, but also makes that reality with its pain and work explicable and therefore more acceptable, reinforcing the very structure whose emergence Eden describes. At the same time the cosmogonic theme with its image of the world as initially and ideally ordered preserves a paradise to recall and retrieve when reality's structures become a source of oppression or anomie or when we, as individuals or societies, feel boxed in by rules set for ourselves which in their stringency are impossible to keep.

In this way the creation myths of Genesis 1–11 provide a means of self-renewal even while preparing us to live in a world of structures and reality. They prepare us for who we are as human beings but also remind us of who we might be.

INDEX OF SCRIPTURAL CITATIONS

GENERAL INDEX